WOULD YOU BUY FROM YOU?

YOUR BRAND MAKES THE DIFFERENCE

RYAN T. SAUERS

Author of *Everyone is in Sales*

Would You Buy from You?

First edition: March 2015

ISBN: 978-0692287712

Table of Contents

Dedication

This book has been a true labor of love and has taken a great deal of time. I have thrown my heart over the fence and let the words follow. I dedicate this book to those special people in my life who have been a "sounding board" each step of the way. You know who you are and I thank you. I praise Jesus Christ as Your grace is indeed "amazing." I could never write a book without the gifts You have blessed me with. Finally, I dedicate this book to my amazing wife and kids. Lara, it is an honor to be your husband. Kelsey, McKenna, and Brooke —you are the best three daughters a guy could ask for. I am so proud of each of you and I am honored to be your father. All of your support in this endeavor means more to me than you will ever know.

iv

ACKNOWLEDGEMENTS:

Would You Buy from You?
Your Brand Makes the Difference

This book has been in the works (in my mind at least) for several years. I learned a lot from writing my first book, and I learned how to do things more effectively in this one. I am thankful to so many individuals around the country and at home who have given me insights over the past few years that I tucked away. You know who you are if you have had to listen to it, and thus realize you played a role in this book.

This book took over a year to write, and its title and subject were modified along the way. There is no such thing as just *writing* a book; *rewriting* the book is where most of the time is spent. I am confident these pages will help us look at things we may know on some level in new ways, and to think about the world we live in, what it means in 2015 and beyond, and what this means to sales and marketing.

I want to thank Glen, Mark, Jay, Ted, Kim, Erik, Vern, Richard, and many others for your insights. I am thankful for the many opportunities I have had to share pieces of this book with clients, university classes, and speaking audiences. In doing so, I was able to see what made sense and what did not. A special thanks to the editorial team and designers Elsie, Steve, Lorrie, and Catherine. You all are amazing. Thanks so much to my family, friends, and colleagues for your support of this endeavor. It means a lot.

Thank you to my terrific wife and three wonderful daughters. I love you all more than you will ever know. Thanks for putting up with my talking about this book for the past year. And finally, I thank my Creator, Redeemer, Savior, and Lord – Jesus Christ. Thanks for letting me play a small role (with this book) in Your universe.

Ryan T. Sauers, Author, *Everyone Is in Sales* and *Would You Buy from You?*

INTRODUCTION:

Would You Buy from You?

My last book, *Everyone is in Sales,* was written three years ago. I reframed the word "sales" to "communications" to convey how we all try to "persuade" others with our messages so they can see things from our vantage point. I explained that sales was not about shortcuts, gimmicks, power handshakes, body mirroring, or name repetition. Sales is a genuine endeavor, and it's all about listening, ethics, integrity, passion, and more. That book, which applied to everyone since in some part of life we all are in sales, showed how to adapt individual communication styles to best meet the needs of the intended audience so you can achieve optimal results.

Everyone is in Sales led me all over the country, and I gave many speeches on the subject. Over time, I began to see patterns emerge in every audience and in each region of the country. People are being asked to do more and more in their lives. However, they do not get any more time or hours to get these "things" done. They are overloaded with content, stimuli, and information. Quite frankly, the stress levels of many are really high. People are, as we will cover in Section 1 of this book, constantly connected. I often ask if the "smart phone" was both the best and worst invention of all time in relation to one's life and one's time. I nearly always get a resounding "yes" to both. I continued to hear, "Ryan, I am swamped, drowning, slammed, buried, covered up, snowed under, running ragged." People would also tell me, "Ryan, I wasn't able to finish the paper, write the report, edit the video, get the website updated, etc." When I would ask why, they would answer that they did not have enough time. You get the idea. I am sure you have said something similar before. Amazingly, every person in each situation had enough time to get things done. However, they did not make time to get things done (We will discuss this later in the book).

I am swamped, drowning, slammed, buried, covered up, snowed under, running ragged.

I do many different things for a living and in life, and once I recognized the same repeated patterns in those with whom I spoke, I realized that this was a book that needed to be written. I saw connections between what I was learning as a doctoral student, what I was observing as a consultant, what I was asked in presentations, what questions were asked of me as a professor, what

the community's feedback was to me as a magazine own-
er, what comments readers of my articles and blog posts
made, what I was seeing in digital media, and what top
executives were wrestling with. It all came together. It
took time to frame this book into sections, make it informative, logical, relevant, and simple.

I found that most people are interested in learning
more about where we are as a society (domestically and
globally), and what the future will look like. In addition,
my audience sought to understand what this new world meant to both sales and marketing. Note: sales and marketing, although generally lumped together, are two differ-

We are at the intersection of sales and marketing, where your brand, your uniqueness, your differentiator, and your creative way merge.

ent things. However, as you see in the graphic on the
front cover of this book, I truly believe we are at the
intersection of sales and marketing, where your brand,
your uniqueness, your differentiator, and your creative
way merge. We all have a brand. It is not optional. And
your brand is not what you say it is, but what others say it
is. Perception is indeed reality in the eye of the beholder.

I also learned some topics or ideas I had shared a year
earlier with a specific industry or audience had been "almost exactly borrowed" (new term) and used by someone who did similar work. People asked me if I was upset.
The answer was no. First of all, "copying/borrowing" is a
sign that you are doing something right if people want

to use your material. Jay Baer, who is an international marketing expert, shares later in the book that there is no such thing as a "secret sauce." And he is right. So, I quit doing anything but being me. I may be a little crazy, but at least I am not boring.

Furthermore, there is no such thing as a new idea as it relates to human communication, sales, or marketing. Quite frankly, every idea builds upon the work that came before it. People can copy your ideas. People can copy your thoughts. People can copy your words. But, guess what? They do not have your DNA and can never be YOU. Only you can be you. Is that not liberating? Your only competition is yourself.

The entire idea of this new book came down to a question that I asked hundreds of times these past few years to all levels in a variety of organizations, and it is simple: *Would You Buy from You?* And, generally, the answer I get is, "Hum, uhhhh, well... yes. I mean... I guess I would, Ryan. What do you mean exactly?" Or, "It depends on what I am selling, or how competitive the market is, or what my territory would be." Time out. What? Friends, let me cut to the chase. If you wouldn't—absolutely and unequivocally—buy from you, then why in the world would anyone else buy from you? The answer is that they would not...and will not.

I write from a unique vantage point. I am in my early 40s, sandwiched between the Boomers and Millennials, both large and talented generations. Generation X, my generation, is quite small in comparison. Thus, I appreciate and use traditional sales and marketing methods, in addition to new communication tools. I believe in integrated communications and marketing. In today's world people need to be touched seven to eight times in a variety of ways just to notice you—assuming that you approach them in a creative manner with useful information. My doctoral studies in Organizational Leadership quickly made me realize that there were many

In today's world people need to be touched seven to eight times in a variety of ways just to notice you.

things I thought "I knew," but then soon realized I had not actually thought about them at the deepest level. Early in the program I was challenged to write a paper and defend my worldview. I figured this would be a relatively simple paper since I know what I believe. And, as a Christian, I thought this was a pretty simple answer. Wow, was I wrong. They asked me to not only share what my worldview was, but also to carefully and logically defend each reason I espoused and what I believed in. It was at this moment in time that I came to understand deep "why" level thinking. You see, they were helping me get to my "why" level; but I was still thinking at the surface level. I came to understand that these topics, when shared with the vast majority of people in my life, were not connecting, because either people did not understand or want to understand, or they did not care. The information was too academic—not broken down into a practical and applicable way that people could easily process, grow from, learn, and improve. So, I began taking critical pieces of information from a variety of sources and breaking them down in new ways. The results and feedback were amazing. I changed the terms and simplified things, and people loved it. For me, an iceberg became an example of a worldview.

In sales, we tend to focus and discuss surface-level matters (what we can see), which are the "whats and hows." However, this above-the-surface part of the iceberg makes up only 10 percent of it. We are guilty of failing to delve deeper (under the surface) to understand the "why"—which makes up 90 percent of the iceberg. In sales and marketing, we tend to focus on what is visible and right in front of us. We often take things literally and fail to understand the true reason a buyer is saying, "No. Not now. Go away," or "I am not interested." Theory is fine, but what happens in the real world is what makes all the difference. So in this book you will find practical applications you can utilize in your life and business.

The rapid change of our world can be viewed through a *PEST* model. P stands for *Political*. In the United States and around the world there is a great amount of discontent in the political arena, whether local or national. People are completely divided as to which way things should be and where things should go in the future. I am sure you know what I mean, and I will leave it at that. E stands for *Economic change*. In the past eight years we have seen some of the worst financial times since the great depression. People lost jobs, homes, savings, and more.

S stands for *Social trends*. Societal demographics are more diverse than at any time in recent history. In addition, we have five distinct generations in society. Some argue it is four. I break up the fourth one that many call the Millennials into Generation Y and Millennials. Why? One generation grew up with the internet, and the one after grew up with a mobile device in hand.

A person is not an age any more than he or she is a skin color, gender, or religion.

In addition, we have four generations in the work force for the first time ever. I am repeatedly asked, "Ryan, how do we deal with these young people?" or, "How do we understand those older people?" The answer is simple. A person is not an age any more than he or she is a skin color, gender, or religion. In contrast, they are persons with unique qualities, and they can learn a lot from both the generation ahead and the one behind.

Finally, T stands for *Technological*. We have had more changes in technology in the past fifteen years than most can comprehend. Think about it for a moment. IPad and tablets, DVRs, smart phones, texting, social media, WIFI, GPS, E-books, instant music downloads, streaming movies…the list goes on and on. We can barely learn one technology before something new comes out. The change is amazing, powerful, unprecedented, and, at times, overwhelming. When the PEST model perspective is used, it becomes evident that we are experiencing change that has never been seen before in all four areas at the same time.

In Section 3 of the book, we discuss branding, which will be covered in great detail. As it says in the title, "Your brand makes the difference." What does this mean? Your brand is everything that you stand for online and offline. If I asked a person in Charleston, South Carolina, if they know (fictitious) Bob Jenkins, they could answer two ways assuming they knew Bob and were able to refrain from saying something negative. First, they could say, "Yes, I know Bob." They could also say, "Oh, my goodness. Bob Jenkins. Man, that guy is as good as gold. When I hurt my back, he mowed my yard the entire year. What a great person." The interesting part is that the first response said nothing bad about Bob Jenkins; yet it told a whole lot about him as well. The second response did not have to say as much as it did, but it makes me want to meet Bob Jenkins.

We will examine branding in a methodical manner: what it is, what it means, why it matters, and how to grow your own brand in a consistent manner online and offline. So think of the word *CUB* as a method to remember the main ideas of this book. C is for *Constantly Connected*; U is for *Under the Iceberg*; and B is for your *Brand*.

Trust takes a long time to build and can be destroyed in an instant.

In the conclusion we will take everything we have learned and break it down into final takeaways. For example, trust is a key reason you buy from anyone, are friends with anyone, or share confidential things with

8

anyone. It is the glue that creates a bond between two human beings. Trust takes a long time to build and can be destroyed in an instant.

So, friends, let's get to it. I encourage you to embrace this book with an open mind, with what I call an "as if" (it could be done now) mindset, and plow into the question of *Would You Buy from You?* Then, at the end of this book, you will see the question change to "How Could You Not Buy from You?"

SECTION I:

CONSTANTLY CONNECTED

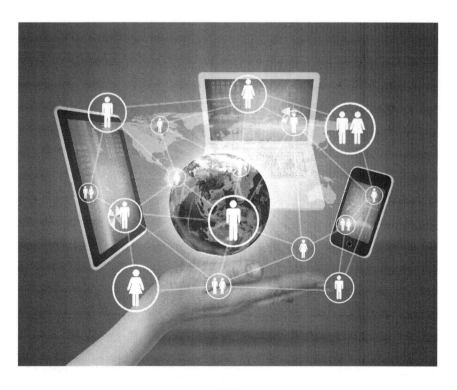

CHAPTER 1:

The NEW Information Overload

Section 1 will play a big role in helping you rethink the world we live in, and thus how we can be most successful in our sales efforts. Let's get to it.

In today's world, we are generally expected to accomplish more in the same or less amount of time than we did in years past. The unprecedented amount of information that bombards us

The unprecedented amount of information that bombards us with each passing hour, day, and week is overwhelming.

with each passing hour, day, and week is overwhelming. This is more than information overload; it's the *new* information overload. Our society is constantly connected

13

with Internet access, text messaging, emails, and more. If we desire to disconnect from this world, we have to make a conscious, deliberate effort.

We live in a globally connected world that is 24/7 and never stops.

How did we get here? Wasn't the goal of all of our technological advances to make our lives easier? So let me ask, does technology work for you, or do you work for it? We live in a globally connected world that is 24/7 and never stops. And, it seemingly gets faster each year. Think about how long it took human beings to communicate to the masses. It began with newspapers, then radio, then television, and now it occurs through the unfiltered, globally connected, nonstop social networks. The "information" can be of great or little value, yet we still must find a way to deal with it and thus balance our time.

People tell me they wish things would slow down so they could catch their breath. Many are stressed to the max. Books have been written about information overload, balance, and/or the "margin" in one's life. A favorite book of mine, *Margin*, written by Richard Swenson M.D. in 1994, made a number of true and excellent points on this subject, even though the book was written more than two decades ago. And things have gotten even faster in this mobile and digital media era. So, what does a curious fellow like me do? I contacted Dr. Swenson to get his take on things more than twenty years later. Richard shared, "Margin is the space between our load and our limits. Unfortunately, as progress gives us more and more of everything faster and faster, our margin grows smaller. Eventually, this hyper dynamic nature of progress collides with our relatively fixed human limits, placed within us by God. We all have, for example, emotional, physical, relational, financial, and time limits. If we live carelessly, these limits will be routinely overwhelmed by the relentless profusion of progress. Margined, maximized, or overloaded. Choose well, for there are wide-ranging consequences to how we live."

Wow. He nailed it. You can see why he is a bestselling author and doctor. We have made amazing progress due to technology, but at what cost? Where does it end, and when will things slow down? Has such "speed" caused our relationships or health to suffer? How much connectivity is too much? My colleague and marketing expert, Erik Equalman, tweeted the following poignant statement: "Keeping your eyes on your computer screen or flipping open your cell sends the message that your child's words aren't important." This is so true. I have a tendency— ask my wife and kids—of quickly becoming annoyed when people glance at their phones when I am talking to them. However, I struggle to keep from doing the same thing to others when they are talking to me. Sales 101 tells us this is terrible to do since we should be actively engaged with the person we are communicating with. The person across from you is the most import-

The person across from you is the most important thing at that moment in time, not your smart device.

ant thing at that moment in time, not your smart device. When I train salespersons, I now tell them to turn off their phones, or leave them in the car.

Why do you think so many people are saying, "I am so ready for the weekend or the next holiday"? Simple. They want this "bad" part of connectivity to stop so they can slow down and rest or catch up on things. Most of us love the "good parts" of our on-demand world—those that allow us to get what we want, when we want it, and where we want it. For example, think about how we used to go to Blockbuster to browse the selections and rent a movie. Over time, this became slow, and the process was improved and expedited with the advent of Netflix. You did not have to leave your home to get a movie. You preselected choices that were placed in your video queue. When you mailed a movie back, your next one was mailed to you. In time, this too became "slow" as movies became available on demand to watch any place, any time, and on any device. Many people do not watch movies on their televisions. They stream them to their computer, tablet, or phone. I see this frequently among the youngest generation, which I call the *DVR generation*. One day I was watching a live football game with my youngest daughter. She asked me to fast forward through the commercials, and I told her I could not. When she asked why, I told her the game was live. She responded, "So, why can't you forward it?" True story.

Take connectivity a step further: we have the advent of Google's Chromecast and Amazon's Fire TV. You have a stick, you put it in a HDMI port, and you can then stream on-demand movies, shows, music, and more without having cable or a satellite feed. Again, let me stress there are good and bad things with all of these changes. Walt Disney said, "Times and conditions change so rapidly that we must keep our aim constantly focused on the future." I concur with Mr. Disney.

As we journey through this book to ultimately understand, reflect, and develop answers to the question, *Would You Buy from You?* please remember that all of this stimuli affects the selling, marketing, and buying process. Sales

> *Relationships take time to build, but it is imperative to remember that we have all become programmed to "want things yesterday."*

and marketing professionals know relationships take time to build, but it is imperative to remember that we have all become programmed to "want things yesterday." In the words from the Queen song, *I Want It All,* this line sums us up as consumers in this new world: "I want it all, I want it all, I want it all…and I want it now."

We used to go to the bookstore to look for a book, and if it was not in stock, the bookseller would order it for us. And we were happy with that. With the advent of Amazon and other online bookstores, our expectations have dramatically changed. We complain when we have to wait a couple of days or even overnight for a book to ship to us. This is the new "slow." Maybe you are reading this on an e-book. These devices allow us to read books at the click of a button. We can now download a book instantaneously and begin to read it in a matter of minutes. I must admit this is something I love (As a side note, I will never forget a book signing—yes, of hard copy books— where I was asked how I would sign an electronic copy of my book. I thought the person was kidding, but he was not. I still do not have an answer for that one!).

Do you remember how slow the speed of the Internet was a decade ago, and yet we loved it? Then the mystery wore off, and we wanted faster speeds. In 2015, it seems none of us have the patience to wait a few extra seconds for the Internet to connect. And man, can you remember a time before WIFI? A world or place without WIFI is no good, right? Yes, we indeed, "…want it all… and want it now."

In today's working world, I doubt most people ever truly get "away from the office." Why? They have, over time, become programmed to always be accessible. Even when they are on a vacation or off for the weekend— which used to mean the end of the work week—they are still connected somehow to the office. Before mobile phones, an employee had a home landline, and that was it. Before email existed, you would leave for the day, the weekend, or a vacation, and unless the office really needed you or you wanted to call and check in, voila, you were disconnected. The most connected you would be was to have a pager (Ouch! Did I just say that?), and if someone really needed you, then they would "page" you so you could call them on a payphone. Today, we have clients sending quotes to salespersons over the weekend via text message. I have people telling me that they are scared to take time away for fear of getting behind. And some don't ever take a vacation. They tell me it is just not worth it. Are you catching all this? This is how much our world has changed.

So what about 2015? Your job description may not say you have to do this, but this staying constantly connected (emails and texts at all hours, etc.) is the new norm. We are tied to these devices like a magnet with all the information (and more) that a huge computer from 15 years ago could provide, and yet, our heads hurt, our eyes ache, and our backs are sore from so much "online time." What do we do when we are bored? My new default is looking at my little buddy, the Smart Phone. He can (yes, with a wife and three daughters, it is a "he") navigate where I need to go, keep up with my to-do list, calendar, emails, texts, and social media, stream sports, tell me places to eat, play music, play videos, display books, search the Bible, and much more. Man, this "friend" is amazing. However, this friend now feels like an appendage that I would feel lost without. The goal is to disconnect, in some manner, so we can reconnect with others.

The goal is to disconnect, in some manner, so we can reconnect with others.

So, maybe this is why we feel that we never get any downtime. We don't make time to rest and disconnect. The first thing many people do when they wake up each day is look at their smart phone. And, the last thing they

19

do at night before they go to bed is look at their smart phone. Could that be overloading our thinking?

As you continue to read, think about our world as I describe it and how these examples help you to address the question of this book, *Would You Buy from You?* First, you should see a theme. Things change. Things are changing fast. And things will continue to change even faster, even though we cannot go any faster as human beings. I don't know about you, but no matter how quickly I try to work, and how much I try to squeeze into each day, like Dr. Swenson said before, I have set limits of what can be done. And so do you.

People used to go to music stores to buy albums, records, or cassette tapes, and like books and movies, if they were out of stock, you were out of luck. And, we had to wait. Yes, wait! Enter the advent of digital music where there is no need to wait since you can download your desired song in seconds. Can you see how this affects our patience and expectations when we desire to buy something? How much are consumers paying attention to a marketing message? How well are they listening to a sales presentation? The more technology develops, the more information there is to consume or sort through, and the shorter our attention span becomes.

The more technology develops, the more information there is to consume or sort through, and the shorter our attention span becomes.

I asked my friend, bestselling author Mark W. Schaefer, about this subject. He offered a nice twist on this, referring to what we are experiencing as *content shock*. Mark shared, "By 2020, the amount of information on the Internet is expected to increase by 500% (and some people think that is a low estimate). So let's get our heads around that. If you can imagine the vastness of the Internet you know today, in a few years, there will be at least five of those. This is good news for consumers, because more content means more choice. But this development will pose a significant challenge for businesses trying to reach through that wall of noise to stay connected to their customers. That's the content shock many businesses will be facing. Competing in this environment will require new ideas, new strategies, perhaps even a bigger marketing budget to retain our mindshare with customers."

Friends, this insight provides a great way to think about the entire idea of this section. We can talk about how the world is or used to be, but you know, "it is what it is." I don't really like that expression, but it is the best one I can think of. However, people are still people no matter what changes are going on, and thus the personal connection makes a huge difference. I call this *H2H Sales* (Human-to-Human Sales). All this connectivity may be great or bad, but the personal touch still matters. It matters a lot, and "real world relationships" can never be replaced by online ones.

I often tell salespersons that this is the best time in history to be selling. I tell them that they have more information and ways to contact buyers than any salesper-

> *Someone is going to get the sale and new client. Will that person be you?*

son in any era. The only reason not to like this is if you do not use connectivity properly, you focus on the wrong things, or you lose sight of the personal touch. So, you should be excited. Someone is going to get the sale and new client. Will that person be you?

The second some people finish running or cycling, they post their time to social networks so others will know what they did and when. An avid runner recently told me that she fell down because she was looking at her phone while running. Huh? What is going on? Another person shared that he got seriously injured at the gym while looking at his phone. A couple of months ago, I got a taste of my own medicine. I was walking into a restaurant with my family while looking at my phone. Since I was not paying attention, I stepped off the curb sharply and jarred my back. My wife and daughters all looked at me with the same expression and word, "Really? And you are writing a book that touches on this subject, right?" I never professed to be an expert as I am learning along with the rest of you; but I am indeed your tour guide, so I am trying to keep this as real as possible.

Here are some positives about being constantly connected. During last year's March Madness (college basketball tournament), my alma mater (undergraduate) Mercer Bears upset the Duke Blue Devils in basketball. This was an amazing moment. However, what was even more fun was that a number of my college friends and fraternity brothers were communicating in real time thru a multitude of mediums while watching, sharing, and cheering for this remarkable achievement. In another example, what about the ALS Ice Bucket challenge with people dumping ice buckets of water over their heads? Donating money to ALS and educating them about this illness was amazing. It was fun. It went viral, and it raised millions (for a great cause), all because we are constantly connected. You see, there are new ways to sell and market. And, ALS was able to raise a lot of money because we are so constantly connected. I share all of this because you must understand where we have been, where we are, and where we are headed in order to add true value and to answer the question of this book.

Have you ever seen people missing the sunset because they are taking "selfies" or photos to post online? Instead of talking to our dinner partners, we are surfing our smart phone. Maybe we should date our smart phone. At funerals or weddings, people are taking pictures of old friends they have caught up with and posting those photos online. They are focused on the external audience, not the one in front of them. Have you ever seen the mad dash of people grabbing their phones when an airplane lands? It sounds like an arcade with every beep and chime going off at the same time. Goodness, we may have missed a text, phone call, email, or tweet in that two-hour flight. Again, I too struggle with this and try my hardest to resist the temptation to see "what I missed" and rush madly to reconnect through all my channels (since I was disconnected from them for a couple hours). Of course, to truly disconnect, I often choose not to use the plane's WIFI, and instead use this flying time to rest and think.

This constantly-connected lifestyle is not limited to social media. It is in everything. Try finding a quiet place. Where is it? The beach, lake, mountains, farm, desert? Why do you think these places sounds like paradise to so many of us? The answers are much the same. They are all quiet, restful, and peaceful for the most part. We are trying, whether we realize it or not, to get away from it all, and the funny thing is, this forces us in many cases not to have smart phone reception. Coincidence? I doubt it. We become disconnected, catch

> *It was liberating to know that I had a break, and could not be reached for a few days.*

our breath, and are in the here and now. We love the technological/on-demand things we have at our fingertips, but when we really desire to decompress, we go to the things that God made: nature, ocean, countryside, fishing, hunting, mountains, etc. I wrote some of this book while aboard a cruise ship sailing in international waters. It was liberating to know that I had a break, and could not be reached for a few days. When I went back to work, I sold better, marketed more effectively, and used my time more wisely. All any of us need is a chance to—in computer terms—reboot.

CHAPTER 2:

It is All About TIME

When I wrote my last book three years ago, I had 20-plus different ways to communicate with someone. In 2015 it is closer to 30-plus ways to communicate. And I am referring to communication mediums I actively use and keep up with (there are many more available beyond this). We must realize that we do not gain more time each week because of more options to connect. Can we communicate faster? Yes. Can we connect to almost anyone at any time on the globe? Yes. Is this good? In some cases the answer is absolutely. The five testimonials on this book's back cover were written by extremely talented and globally-known marketing experts who are also some of the nicest people you would want to meet. And guess what? I would not have known any of them in "real life" without an initial social media connection.

This is where it begins—and when done right—leads to a personal connection.

It is more the norm these days to hear people say, "I am slammed, swamped, running ragged, in the weeds, covered up, drowning, buried, etc." And it is common to hear, "I have not had the time to do xyz." We all have 24 hours a day and 7 days a week. This is—I know you math whiz folks already had this—168 hours in a week. Nobody has any more or any less. You cannot make more time. When people say that they did not *have* time to do xyz, I tell them they did not *make* time to do xyz.

Time is the great equalizer for all mankind—the level playing field for everyone.

Time is the great equalizer for all mankind—the level playing field for everyone. Time does not care about your gender, race, creed, or age, or how much money you have. It does not care what house you live in, how many degrees you have, what your title at work is, how many kids you have, or where you work. Time is our most precious commodity, although many of us never take time (no pun intended) to reflect on this. If we are late and miss 30 minutes of a meeting—there is no way we can ever get that time back.

As an example, you are reading this book now and thus have chosen to do so instead of doing something else. I personally think reading this book was a good call on your part, but, hey, maybe I am biased. In all seriousness, our time is a gift, and what we do with it is a choice. My belief is simple. If you want something badly enough, then you will find *a way* to get it done; and if you don't, then you will find *an excuse*.

The world is full of people who say, "I could've, should've, would've." But this is not proactive behavior, and it is full of excuses. Behind every problem lies a solution. And behind each obstacle lies an opportunity. We have a choice (for the most part) on everything we do and where every hour of our day goes. We choose to let our kids do many activities, we choose to work late hours, we choose to stay at the job we hate, we choose to read a book and not exercise. You can see that nearly everything we do with our time is a choice. We choose to take an existing client to lunch and not prospect for new clients. We choose to do customer service work when we should be at a networking event to meet new people. We choose to watch television at night when we really need to spend time with our kids. It is all our choice.

> *Behind every problem lies a solution. And behind each obstacle lies an opportunity.*

There are three types of salespersons I work with: the *Make Things Happen* salesperson, the *Watch Things Happen* salesperson, and the *Wonder What Happened* salesperson. Now that you have had a chance to laugh, let's briefly discuss what this means, and then you can determine what category you fall into as a salesperson. The Make Things Happen salesperson is the person who finds a way even when the situation looks impossible. This person never stops when an obstacle pops up, and gives every ounce of energy he or she has to make any situation work. This person brings solutions to the table, and is creative, unique, and determined in his or her approach.

The Watch Things Happen salesperson is in the next category. These individuals are cautious and like to observe the situation and reflect on it before making a decision. This group of salespersons often spends a lot of time telling me why things won't work, what they have tried in the past, and what problems they see with xyz. I call this *paralysis by analysis,* because at some point you must pull the trigger. It is the equivalent of getting your car out of neutral and putting it into drive. There is nothing wrong with analyzing a situation, but it is your job to make things happen—not make excuses as to why people are not buying what you are selling.

The third group consists of the Wonder What Happened salespersons. This group is really hard to deal with. They are oblivious to what is going on around them, or they may not care. They spend their time doing the same things they have always done (most times these are things that no longer work), expecting a different result. These people tell me they "don't get social media," and don't see it having value in sales. Huh? We are in 2015. I have seen a few people turn themselves around in this group, but many times they have checked out and are no longer willing to listen, learn, and grow.

From the *Would You Buy from You?* perspective, I would buy from a Make Things Happen salesperson who is realistic, does not "shoot and then aim," and has amazing passion. This is one I would trust. This person will stop at nothing to be the best at what he or she does, making my life as a customer much easier in the process. These people will solve problems for me that I don't have time to look at or have not thought to consider. And as a result, this is a person I would indeed

> *Social media is no longer something we try to make part of our real world. In actuality, it is part of everything we do and read and where we go.*

buy from, so this person gets a resounding *yes*. We all need to strive to become Make Things Happen salespersons in all that we do so we can all hear the word *yes!*

My *Everyone is in Sales* book had a chapter entitled "Integrating Social Media into the Real World." Now three years later, that chapter would need a different name. Social media is no longer something we try to *make* part of our real world. In actuality, it *is* part of everything we do and read and where we go. It has become a cornerstone of our use of time and how information is spread, how news gets out, and what recommendations are given. Do you realize that news used to break from traditional media outlets as they were out hounding their sources or interviewees for quotes, stories, etc.? Today, it is much different. News breaks on social media channels, and it's picked up by traditional news media. Blogs and other social media tools allow a politician, athlete, celebrity, and, more importantly, *any* person to share what they want to say to the world in an "unfiltered manner." Thus, we often find traditional media outlets quoting Tweets, Facebook posts, blog posts, and more. There is no filter in 2015 and beyond.

Recently, Tiger Woods took exception to a parody article a golf journalist had written about him. http://www.golfchannel.com/news/golf-central-blog/woods-angry-jenkins-parody-pens-essay/ Guess what? He did not call a news conference or break the story thru a selected journalist. Instead, he blogged his response to this situation, and it was immediately picked up by media outlets and shared throughout the world. It is not even debatable whether the social world is here to stay, or if social media is some fad. It is here to stay, and in our *Would You Buy from You?* way of thinking, social media plays an enormous role in how you build your brand and how you socially sell.

And by the way, don't get caught up on the names of the tools we use to connect. Those will change the same way Myspace dwindled away, and Facebook changed from a college audience to a much older demographic. As a side note, I have had many people tell me that to them Facebook is social media. This is incorrect. It is simply one social media tool. And, for me, it is at least #4 on my list of most effective social media business tools. When talking about noise and reaching customers, Mark Schaefer said, "We're already seeing change occur in places like Facebook where our ability to reach customers organically is down to nearly zero for most businesses. Why? There is simply too much content, and Facebook has to edit the news stream down to a manageable level—unless you pay them to highlight your content, of course!"

So, you see, changes will keep coming. Although the tools may change, it is the over-arching mindset of communications that I want you to embrace. And your brand online and offline must be the same. They must be consistent and authentic. Anything less and you will be seen as a phony.

Here is another positive. The world of social connections gives anyone, anywhere the opportunity to have his or her voice heard and be an expert. Have you heard the term *YouTube celebrity*? These are people who have such a strong and organic following that they have hundreds of

> *And your brand online and offline must be the same. They must be consistent and authentic.*

thousands (or more) of devoted fans who watch their material. Thus, the music industry looks at such sites to find future stars. Guess what? This, too, is a positive. And, the same holds true for blogging. Top bloggers have tremendous influence in the information they share and the people they influence. If I had not been an early blogger, I would not have learned about, understood, or gotten involved with social media. And without social media, I would not have connected with so many people who I now have real world friendships with. Without social media, I could not have built a brand as easily (remember *your brand makes all the difference*) that people wanted to understand and build a relationship with. This would have limited my speaking, writing, magazine, radio, and TV opportunities. Thus, I have met so many great people in less time than would have ever been possible in the past.

> *However, if you use your ability to connect with anyone/anywhere wisely, then you will ultimately build many new relationships.*

I can tell you that I would not be doing what I am doing today without such tools. And, I can promise you I would not have written a first book much less a second book without them. Utilizing all of these communication tools does require a commitment of time, but it is very doable. We are in a chapter about time and only have so much of it. However, if you use your ability to connect with anyone/anywhere wisely, then you will ultimately build many new relationships. And, yes, ultimately sell more.

With 168 hours of time each week, how much of it is productive connectivity and how much is wasted time? Do you know or even think about this? Trust me; I am speaking to myself here as much as I am to you. No matter what your answer is, you must think about this concept as we go deeper into the modern sales process in the subsequent sections. You see, folks, what we do with our time is a choice. We can protect it, shelter it, waste it, share it, balance it, invest it, lose track of it, neglect it, use it wisely, etc. And, in my best Bubba voice from *Forest Gump*, "…and that is about all the things we can do with time."

Something else we must consider are the time demands on our families. If your child is heavily involved in an activity, the time demands almost never stop. I have three daughters who play travel soccer. These days, in nearly every competitive activity for children, the season goes nearly year round. As parents, coaches, and kids we have fallen into a trap of feeling compelled to specialize in an activity at an early age or else fear getting passed by. My oldest daughter took off the first season ever from competitive soccer and absolutely loved it. I was so proud of her. She had six months away, and then wanted to come back. She is now rejuvenated, playing high school soccer, and loving it again. My guess is that time away made her fall in love with what had become a ball-and-chain obligation that was no longer fun. As you can see, this total focus of time on one thing leads to many injuries and to burnout. Forgetting all of that, these children will be tomorrow's salespersons, marketers, and buyers.

I mentioned kids' activities, but many of us run at this fast pace in our personal lives as we try to make up for the long hours we worked during the week. Thus, the "weekend" is not so restful, and we come back to work more tired than when we left. I share these things because this is the mindset we must explore and understand as we seek to sell to a buyer who was "slammed" over the weekend with kids or personal stuff, who is pulled in ten directions at work, and who is trying to balance many other components of his or her life. So, think about it. How attentive do you think buyers are to your voice-mail about wanting to come by to meet them? I have listened to a lot of the voice-mails salespersons leave for buyers. I have read a lot of salespersons' emails. And, I have listened to a lot of first and subsequent contact calls. Many of them are weak and lacking. We talk about our stuff, our company, our offerings, our availability, and our years in business; and like the sound an adult in a Charlie Brown cartoon makes, we hear, "WHAH WHAH WHAH WHAH."

> *We talk about our stuff, our company, our offerings, our availability, and our years in business; and like the sound an adult in a Charlie Brown cartoon.*

You likely say much the same thing as everyone else: you offer good customer service, top quality, and competitive pricing. So, why would they want to meet with you, much less buy from you when they are already struggling to find one more hour in their day? The only way they will give up their precious time to return your message (much less meet with you) is if you have a unique approach that brings value to the sales process. Here are some things to consider. Can you bring them some ideas that will save them time? Can you provide them with answers they did not have time to look up? Can you make them look good to their boss? Can you provide them headache relief? Can you bring creative solutions that will make their lives easier?

To help us think about this subject of *TIME*, I created an acronym that will be helpful as we go through this book. And remember, this entire book is focused on how we build our brand to sell more

> *We are totally inundated with multiple media every moment of every day.*

and market better. The acronym is: ***Total Inundation Multimedia Every day.*** What does this mean? We are totally inundated with multiple media every moment of every day. Quite frankly, if you don't deliberately find a place to unplug and disconnect, then disconnect will not happen.

I recently asked some Facebook friends the following question: Is lack of time your greatest frustration, and if you had more time to do what you wanted, would you be happier? Fifty-five responses came back *affirmative. Yes!* I have also confirmed this at more than sixty speeches I have given. In each speech, I ask everyone to take a deep breath and blow it all out and relax. And then I ask how they feel. Everyone generally laughs and says, "It is so nice to just *be.*" When did just "be" become the exception rather than the rule? Last time I checked, we were called human *beings* and not human *doings.* Yet most of us have a very hard time sitting still and *being.*

A friend of mine, Dennis Smock, has written a daily devotional that I have read for many years entitled

Be Still...Devotionals for Daily Living https://dailyliv-ingministries.wordpress.com/ taken from Psalm 46:10. This Scripture really speaks to me. If we were created in God's image, then how is it that we cannot stand to be still? Are we scared? Do we not like what we see? Are we bored? Do we crave constant stimulation? And yes I struggle with this as well.

Recently, I was reminded by my pastor that Jesus did not call Himself the great "I will be" or the great "I was" but instead the great "I Am." If this is what the God of the universe says (present focused) with I Am, then why are we continually looking backward (past tense) or forward (future tense)? Yesterday is good to remember, learn from, appreciate, and reflect on. There is nothing wrong with that. However, I see many people spending most of their time "in the past" and longing for what could have been or what didn't happen. Many may have pain, regrets, or memories that are keeping them in the past. For example, consider the 45-year-old guy who relives his high school athletic achievements and glory days over and over. News flash: What you are doing with your life *now* matters more than what happened some 30 odd years ago...that you are still talking about. Reminiscing is fine, but living in the past is not good.

> *What you are doing with your life* now *matters more than what happened some 30 odd years ago.*

In contrast, some people live in the future. They like to say, "Someday I'll do this or do that." They dream about how nice life could be once they "retire" from the job they hate. To these people the future is better than the now. Ouch. So am I saying we should not plan and dream? Absolutely not. However, if you have a great vision for the future, the only way to achieve it is to begin using

What are you doing today that will prepare you for the future?

your time today in a deliberate and methodical manner. What are you doing today that will prepare you for the future? What lessons do you need to learn now that you will need to draw from in the future? In our constantly connected world, there is never the *right* time or *enough* time to do something. So why not begin today?

Recently, I was speaking to a high-level executive about doing consulting work for his company. The issue was not our price, the value my firm would bring, or the fact that his company needed help. This was the gist of the conversation in December. "Ryan, we do want to work with you. We need your firm's help. But let me share with you the dilemma so you can see how our year looks. January is not good as we are all slammed and getting back into the swing of things from the holidays. February is much the same and when we really need our people freed up to sell. March and April are tough months for us as it is the beginning of spring and a lot of our people take time off especially due to the different spring break schedules. May is not the best due to the end of school and the Memorial Day holiday. The summer months are slow for us, and as it is summer, we have a lot of people off depending on the week. August is back-to-school time so our team is more focused on that than anything else. Labor Day plays a big role in September as it is the last getaway weekend before the cold season begins, and the first family break after school has started…and of course football season has begun. Ryan, you know, October may be good. However, November is a short month that has Thanksgiving, and you know December is impossible with the holidays, year-end, etc…"

I was silent when he finished, then simply said, "So based on what you just told me, and although you all agree you are in dire need of help and that this is a good fit, the only month we could do work together is October." I felt like saying, "What about Halloween? I am sure that will be tough to overcome." There is always a reason not to do *something*—decision by indecision—or to continually stare at the same data and do *nothing*. This is paralysis by analysis.

> *The desire to change has to be so great to an individual that he or she will make time for it to happen.*

The desire to change has to be so great to an individual that he or she will make time for it to happen. No excuses. They know that they will go through a "valley of despair" before the change gets better. What does this mean? When change begins, everyone is excited as there is a lot of early momentum. However, there will be setbacks, frustrations, and more, and things will "get worse/harder" before they get better. We must be willing to endure tough times in the change process to receive the benefits (when things are better) in the end.

Let's say you want to lose 25 pounds. The first two weeks you lose 2.5 pounds, the third week you do not lose any weight, and the fourth week you gain a half pound. You are exercising, eating better and less, and drinking more water. Are most people frustrated at this point? You bet. How many people quit at this point? Some. How many say, "I will do this one more week, and if I am not down in weight, I am done with this"? Many. It is the few who will make things happen, who will set their minds to a goal, who will have a proper plan in place, that will know things will work out (in the end) if they follow the plan. They don't measure their weight every hour or day, but stay focused on the bigger picture. The weight-loss analogy is identical to change initiatives that happen with our consistent dedication to improving sales and marketing. We must put time into the endeavor and be fully invested in it.

For change to occur (weight loss), people must embrace the concept of the bigger picture, the greater good, and staying the course. Is this difficult? Yes, it is very difficult. It is harder than ever to bring about lasting and meaningful change when everyone desires "instant results." This is the identical issue we deal with as salespersons who are trying to differentiate ourselves. Many of us just give up after a couple of contacts, or get distracted, or fall behind.

You have heard of the elevator speech, where you should be able to explain who you are or what you do in

> *Brevity is the new norm for the constantly connected human being.*

the time it takes an elevator to ride from the bottom to the top, etc. Well, I argue that this is more time than most will give you on an elevator or elsewhere. In the event someone is actually listening to you, you have about 12 seconds to make an impact. The shorter the better. Brevity is the new norm for the constantly connected human being. So you ask, "What should I say on an elevator ride?" Something short, simple, and creative (think tweet).

A person on an elevator may ask me, "Ryan, what do you do?" Well, if I was not aware of the human condition or even the older rules of an elevator speech, I might try to blab on and on that I am a speaker, consultant, professor, etc. Uhhhh. No good, and boring since they do not care. Instead, I say, "My business is growing your business." And what else do I say? Nothing. I shut up! Pause. Be quiet. You get the idea.

I have just "pinged the ball" over to them, and if I have at all peaked their attention with a very short snippet of information, they might ask, "So, are you like an ad agency?"

From this point I can say, "No, we are not an agency, but we focus on helping our clients perform at a higher level on the front side of their business." And I shut up. Pause. Be quiet. You notice that each statement is powerful, short, and sufficient enough to hold their attention over their group text chat, Facebook feed, and email.

From there they may likely ask, "What services do you offer?" My response would be, "If you could use front-in help with any part of your business, what would it be?" And I shut up again. From there they might say they are struggling with their social media presence or their business development, etc. Bingo! I now know a specific area where I can focus, and I can determine how I can meet this need in an intelligent manner.

What makes all of this even more complicated yet exciting is that we have five generations among us right now: the Matures (who I call *the Radio generation*); the Boomers (who I call *the TV generation*); GEN X (who I call *the cable generation*); GEN Y (who I call *the Internet generation*); and the Millennials (who I call *the DVR generation*).

> *Do not make the assumption that a 70-year-old does not text, nor assume that a 15-year-old only texts and never uses the phone.*

I refer to these generations according to the media they grew up with. And, what they grew up with plays a large role in how they interact and communicate today. But let me say this: do not make the assumption that a 70-year-old does not text, nor assume that a 15-year-old only texts and never uses the phone. Yes, there are evidences to the contrary; however, more research is needed to make such a definite statement.

Okay, I will now play the guinea pig. I am in my early 40s and part of GEN X. I grew up watching ESPN and

MTV, and I watched as three main channels exploded into many more. I remember 8-track tapes, cassette tapes, and CDs. However, I now choose to download all my music electronically and instantaneously. I finished college right as the Internet was coming alive. I began my career in sales before email was common. When I looked for sales leads, it was not with Google but at the library or in the Yellow Pages. I fall on the spectrum somewhere between a person in his 60s and a person in his 20s. I have embraced social media and did so early on as I saw this as a new way for human beings to communicate. As I tell everyone, I am not great with electronic devices, but social media is not about such computer devices. Social media is all about communications and relationships (which I am good at), so I got involved. Many of my best career opportunities have come because we have such a connected world. It is amazing for me to see just how easy it is to find anything you want with a few screen touches or mouse clicks.

My family goes to Disney World frequently, and I watch people not enjoying their time together, but doing a "play by play" of every person they are with, of pictures they are in, of everything they are doing, etc. It is like we have all become actors in some type of voyeuristic and global show. Anyone can see without even talking to you where you work, what you think, who you are dating or who you are married to, where you live, what you enjoy, etc. Is this a good thing? This book addresses and examines many such things you may have thought about at some level. It will ask you questions that go deep—not surface-level "what and how" questions, but core-level "why" questions. Why are we all doing this? This will be covered in Section 2.

RYAN T. SAUERS

CHAPTER 3:

Break Through the Noise:
The 9 Cs of Sales

There are 9 Cs that I would like you to consider to help break through the noise of being constantly connected. But before we discuss these Cs of Sales, I want to share a few things that show you how large companies also realize changes must be made in this area. Recently Visa changed its marketing slogan from "It's everywhere you want to be" to "Everywhere you want to be." Why? Visa also realized that a customer's attention span is shorter these days. For instance, why type the word "two" when you can type the number "2"? In short, our noisy world demands a message that is shorter in nature. Visa is changing its traditional commercials as well. The campaign includes print, outdoor, digital, and social media, as well as the hashtag *#everywhere*. Another example is Alka-Seltzer Plus keeping the words "*Oh, what a* *relief it is"* in their campaign and eliminating the *"Plop, plop, fizz, fizz."* (http://www.nytimes.com/2014/01/13/business/media/visa-trims-slogan-to-expand-meaning.html?_r=0)

I want us to focus on *9 Cs of sales* that are vital to our becoming more successful as salespersons and as marketers. They are listed numerically to make them easier to read, remember, and learn. Here we go.

1. Credible: Is everything that you do or your company does credible? Is it above board and done with integrity and ethics? When deciding whom to buy from, people do not have a lot of time to research a person or company to death. This means our own credibility is at stake. Is what you are suggesting or alluding to likely to occur? Without a strong sense of credibility, it is unlikely that you will be selling much of anything, because the person you wish to sell to may wonder if what you are saying is true.

2. Consistent: Is the information you share with the vast amounts of people you come in contact with reliable in nature? Is it unchanging and stable? People buy from people who are consistent. Such people do not get too high or too low. They look at the entire picture and make decisions that are not "knee-jerk" in nature. If you lack consistency in what you say and do (online or offline), you will have a hard time selling anything to anybody.

3. Compelling: Are your story and brand intriguing? Does it grab someone's attention and make them want to know more? A compelling story makes us become emotionally involved in what we are watching or hearing. If we become involved and entranced in a story, it becomes memorable, and having a compelling story is a trait all great brands share. Simply said, if your story and message are not persuasive enough, you have little chance to stand out from everyone else saying much the same thing.

4. Concise: Is the message you are sharing brief in nature? Remember, this world has a short attention span, so your objective is to make your point simply, succinctly, and clearly so that others will actually remember it and be moved by it. This is why people like tweets (140 characters at a time). Simple is better.

5. Committed: People who are committed find ways to break through this noisy world. Those who you are trying to sell to, *or* sell more to, are looking to do business with people who are *100 percent* committed to what they are selling—not *somewhat* or *mostly* committed. I have seen far too many people who come across as somewhat committed to what they are sharing. Trust me, this reveals itself, and it is an immediate red flag to anyone you are talking to. Adidas had an amazing branding campaign in the 2014 World Cup called "*all in or nothing,*" and media tracking reports said they took the lead in real time marketing. **http://www.campaignbrief. com/2014/07/adidas-wins-battle-of-real-tim.html** I loved the message behind the campaign. *All in or nothing.* This sums up what commitment is about and anything less is unacceptable if you desire to be committed.

6. Caring: Do you care? I mean, do you truly care about the person you are selling goods and services to? I know we all care to some extent, but there is a difference in the salesperson who would rather see a client place a job elsewhere if it is in the best interest of the client. You see this type of salesperson cares more about the long term relationship than they do a single project.

> *ABC= Absolutely Be Caring in sales. If you care more about the other person succeeding, you will win in the end as well.*

Anyone can follow the old "ABC" *Always Be Closing* in sales. And this is fine to have as a goal. But caring sales is more valuable. It is still all out and full throttle, yet much better. So, I have changed this to be: ABC= *Absolutely Be Caring* in sales. If you care more about the other person succeeding, you will win in the end as well.

7. Content: What type of information are you sharing with the people you want to sell to? Is it information that will make their life easier? Will it help them improve in their own job? Content is king. And without it you are not even in the game. You should not only be well read about what you are selling, but also should know about: the needs of the company you are selling to, the person you are selling to, the industry they are in, the industry you are in, and the multitude of ways (pros and cons) that one can market a message. This type of content is powerful. It stands out. It makes the difference between making things happen and watching things happen. And, by the way, great content is quickly becoming an "expectation" of buyers in today's world.

8. Character: What is your character about? This is not about being perfect, but being real. Character development occurs each day as we "try" to be better in what we say, how we conduct ourselves, and more. I don't care what age someone is, what gender they are, what creed they are, what national origin they are, what race they are, how much or little money someone has, etc. What I care about (and this is true for those who are buying) is a person's character. In other words, is this person the real deal, or are they full of it and telling me what I want to hear? As I laid out at the beginning, the answer to the title of this book is *Trust*. There can be no trust unless you are dealing with a person of high character who does what is right no matter what the consequences are. And, if this person is wrong they will readily admit it, learn from it, and grow from it.

9. Clarity: Is your message clear? Is it simple? Remember the acronym *KISS: Keep it Simple Stupid.* Keep it ridiculously basic to the point that there is no chance of miscommunication. Since we live in a world that is overwhelmed with information as we have established, then your best chance to be successful in sales is to be extremely clear. So keep it simple, basic, and easy to understand. Short, sweet, and to the point. And make it simple so anyone can follow what you seek to communicate. I have a little bit more on clarity in a few paragraphs so hang tight.

Please think through all of this first section with what I call "as if" thinking; as if what you are reading could be done now. Suspend your thinking for a little while and think back, if you are old enough, to how things used to be. This is not a book to long for the glory days. However, it is a call for us to "rethink our time" and focus our priorities. I like finding things on Google in a half second. I enjoy knowing the weather by looking at my phone, and I like to see breaking news scroll across my screen.

But there must be boundaries. If you are younger, realize that people older than you remember how to communicate in real time; not through emails, texts, snap chat, Instagram, Twitter, etc. This means you must practice your writing, listening, and human relations skills so you can move back and forth between the online and offline worlds. And if you are older you must learn how to become more effective in communicating through the written word of text, email, Twitter, and more.

We often use these less personal mediums for issues that should be handled in a personal manner.

Here is a question to think about. Why have we all, regardless of age, begun to email or direct message co-workers across the room instead of talking to them? Why do we text someone instead of calling them? I think we find it easier to send a brief email or text to avoid a longer conversation (that we feel) we do not have time for. In reality, I find that texts and emails and other such tools are oftentimes misunderstood by the other party. In addition, we often use these less personal mediums for issues that should be handled in a personal manner. So, in many instances this communication backfires and does more damage than good, and ultimately takes more time than if we would have just called or met with the person to begin with.

I see so many people starved for human interaction. They spend their days playing computer games, and engaging in an online fantasy world that is not real. Now let me be clear. As I stated earlier, there is nothing wrong with any online interaction as long as it has some authentic and real world *In Real Life (IRL)* component to it. We are not created to be disconnected, which many of us are as we communicate via electronic words that contain no emotion. I can't tell you how many people I see who literally run into others at airports because they are looking down at their mobile devices. When I was on a subway train a year ago, the train came to a stop in a large metropolitan city. The next thing I knew, a woman screamed. She had been sitting by the door when the door opened at the stop, and in that brief moment someone from outside the train stepped in, grabbed her purse, and ran. Guess what? Not one of us, including me, saw a thing. Why? We were deeply engrossed in our mobile devices, asleep listening to our music, etc. This is scary and sad. It was at this moment I knew that I was called to write something on this subject. Our world is moving rapidly, and our attention span is shorter than ever. I don't know about you, but I have a hard time deciphering the true message from a sea of shortened words and acronyms. We all want to do things faster, quicker, and in

> *Clarity is what gives a string of letters and words a meaning.*

a hurry. Unfortunately, we cannot afford to lose our ability to communicate clearly. Communication is what gets us what we want in the world: jobs, food, relationships, and lifestyles. If you can't communicate in a clear manner, then you will not be effective in life.

Clarity is what gives a string of letters and words a meaning. When you speak to others, whether online of offline, it is vital that the tone you wish to convey is the one that others hear. For instance, when you need a project done in a prompt manner, it is ineffective to use words such as you need it "ASAP" or "soon." These words do not impart a tone of immediacy. In fact, they mean nothing. ASAP or soon is quite subjective. Instead, try "I need it now" or "I need this by 5 p.m. today."

When you communicate, you must be sure your words do not reflect the message that you are angry or upset (unless you actually are!). Clarity is what will keep your clients coming back to you for their needs and will make your communications more effective. It is frustrating to speak to someone and have no clue what he or she said. Humans are inherently social, but our lack of clarity is hampering many businesses.

Do not contribute to this clarity issue. Instead, I challenge you to think of what you want to say before you say it, and ask yourself these questions: What am I trying to say? How am I trying to say it? How would I feel if someone said this to me?

This finishes the first section of the book, an overview of what the world looks like in 2015. We must understand this before we can more effectively sell or market any product, good, or service. As you now know, people want headache relief and solutions to their problems, and they need these solutions to be easy to understand as they are balancing twenty other things. This is what the modern day salesperson must do to provide value in a manner that does not waste time.

Value along with excellent information (or content) is how we overcome the constantly connected world. And, we can use all these tools at our disposal, like them or not, to create opportunities that would never have existed before. We will now move on to Section 2 and examine a person's worldview so we can get to what is the real reason people say what they say and believe what they believe.

SECTION II:

Under the Iceberg Mindset

CHAPTER 4:

Understand a Worldview

We have discussed our constantly connected world in great detail. Why? So we can understand what is going on in the world around us. If we are going to sell more effectively, we must understand the distractions people face in lieu of focusing on our message. With that in mind, this leads us to the second section of the book. I call this an *Under the Iceberg Mindset.* As you now know, we must work even harder to be successful in our sales and marketing efforts due to our noisy and short-attention-span world. I sought real world feedback before coming up with the title of this section. I asked friends on Facebook what the expression "under the iceberg" meant to them. They had no context clues or biased information, so they just answered off the cuff. Some may have realized this was a question I was asking for this book, so the responses were plentiful and very candid. And it helped me a great deal. About half of them nailed what my meaning was for this section's title, while the other half saw it another way (like a person was drowning or trapped). Thus to clarify, an *Under the Iceberg Mindset* is about the (approximate) 90 percent of the iceberg that is under surface that we cannot see; not the 10 percent above the surface that we can see.

Most people focus on the "what or how" surface level in communicating with others. This means we do not go deep enough, ask enough questions, or truly understand where another person is coming from. A person's "why" is what I refer to as a person's *worldview*. So we will spend some time discussing what a worldview is. However, for this book's

> *Most people focus on the "what or how" surface level in communicating with others.*

purpose, please remember that a person's "why" and their "worldview" are used interchangeably.

A worldview is the method and means through which an individual sees the world. A person's worldview is unique and personal in nature. James Sire says, "A worldview is a set of presuppositions which we hold about the basic make up of our world." A worldview, while it may be different among groups, is common in that individuals of various ages, races, and nationalities have one.

A person's view of the world transcends demographics and generations, and is an obstacle that many wrestle with. For example, in examining worldview, most people are certain that something exists beyond them, yet they have not come to terms with what that something might be. John Moore explains, "Your opinion is your opinion, your perception is your perception—do not confuse them with 'facts' or 'truth.' Wars have been fought and millions have been killed because of the inability of men to understand the idea that everyone has a different viewpoint."

Wilhelm Dilthey states, "A worldview is a set of mental categories arising from deeply lived experience which essentially determine how a person understands, feels and responds to what he or she perceives of the surrounding world and the riddles it presents." Are you starting to get a feel for what one's worldview is all about, and why it is so important to understand it in sales and marketing? Good, then we are on the right track.

> *An individual's worldview can be considered the beliefs, values, and assumptions a person has about the world.*

An individual's worldview can be considered the beliefs, values, and assumptions a person has about the world. This outlook is derived from both an individual's genetic predisposition as well as his or her life experience. This is often referred to as *nature and nurture*. Both shape a person's worldview and explain why people see the world the way that they do. For instance, some people may grow up in positive nurturing environments

59

yet still view the world as a distant and/or cold place. In contrast, others grow up in less nurturing, more negative environments yet view the world as being innately warm and friendly. Nature and nurture play key roles in shaping a person's worldview and must be reviewed in tandem. So let's take a timeout right here. Why am I spending all this time on a person's worldview? What does this have to do with a book on sales? I am glad you asked.

Every sales encounter consists of two or more people. One or more are involved on the selling side, and the purchasing side consists of one or more persons as well. Every sales situation is unique. This means that the way in which a seller presents information and the way in which the buyer receives the information

> *Every experience you have had in your life, in some manner, impacts your sales approach or your buying reception.*

(assuming everyone has adhered to Section 1 and is fully paying attention) are in large part based on their worldviews.

Every experience you have had in your life, in some manner, impacts your sales approach or your buying reception. Here is an example. Have you ever met someone for the first time and either immediately liked or disliked him or her? If you think about it, this is a little strange. How can we like or dislike someone in such a short amount of time? It is due to the bias of our worldview. There are certain parts of the country that are more comfortable for us. There are certain accents we best relate to. A person may have gone to the same school that we did. The list can go on forever.

One person in such an encounter usually says something like this to the other person: "You remind me of my best friend I grew up with in Pennsylvania." Or, "You remind me of my favorite cousin who lives in Oregon." How about this? "You look just like a good friend that I went to college with." We have all been in these situations. Thus, if the experiences such as the ones above are positive, then we immediately like another person because our "worldview filter" instinctively tells us that we should. We are not even aware of the reason we feel this way. In contrast, when someone is dramatically different from us or behaves in a manner that we deem inappropriate or wrong, we tend to dislike this person. By thinking through these examples, we begin to realize how powerful our worldview is, yet many never take time to reflect on why we think what we think, say what we say, or do what we do. Our worldview is key to understanding why we buy what we buy, who we hire, who we award projects to, who we have as friends, who we ask to sit on our board, and who we sit next to at our kids sporting events. Is this important? You better believe it. It is a vital component of this book.

The way a person makes sense of the world is exhibited through the worldview that person embraces. Nash defined worldview as a "...conceptual scheme by which we consciously or unconsciously fit everything we believe and... interpret and judge reality." A person's worldview determines how an individual describes his or her world, makes sense of the world, fits into the world, and determines his or her priorities in the world. Every decision a person makes is influenced to some degree by his or her worldview. He went on to say, "It is…rare when the worldviews of two people match in every important detail… this means that even similar worldviews will likely have differences." An individual's worldview influences how a person treats another as well as one's beliefs about honesty and morals.

One of the early papers I wrote in my doctoral program in organizational leadership at Indiana Wesleyan University was on this subject. I was asked to define and explain my worldview. I thought I knew what my worldview was, but when I was asked to really think deeply (under the iceberg) about it and to answer and defend "why I believe what I believe," it proved more difficult than I had anticipated. You see, everything we have seen, heard, and learned impacts the way we view the world. Moreover, where we have lived, who we have been influenced by, what we have listened to, what we have watched, and where we have traveled are all ingredients of our ingrained worldview. One of my friends, professor and author Dr. Vern Ludden, had this to say when I asked him to explain a person's worldview: "A person's worldview consists of the assumptions, both recognized and unrecognized, that shape our thoughts and subsequent actions. Understanding what drives our worldview and the worldviews of other people is essential to understanding differences, disagreements and discord in the workplace, community, and world. When we recognize the conflicts between worldviews, we can use the knowledge to develop more effective strategies for interacting with others."

Did you notice that Dr. Ludden mentioned interacting with others? This is one of the main focus areas of what we do as sales and marketing professionals. If we do not have effective strategies of how to sell or market then we will never achieve the level of success that is possible. A person's "why" or worldview can be considered the filter through which he or she makes a decision. It is how we all make decisions. Moreover, this "moral compass" is what a person uses to help decide what his or her reaction will be to events and circumstances and how decisions are made. Yes, I said *decisions*. This means a buyer's worldview or "why" has a direct impact on the type of marketing that person is most affected by, the type of sales approach that is most appealing to him or her, and the type of business relationship he or she is looking for.

CHAPTER 5:

Stop and Listen

You remember the song we heard in grade school that said, "Stop, look, and listen"? Do you recall the stop, collaborate, and listen song from Vanilla Ice? I think I heard a *yes*. I want to take these two songs and focus on the two common words in each: *stop* and *listen*. These words make up the title of this chapter because I believe we can all benefit from them. We discussed the importance of stopping or slowing down and becoming aware of both our own and others' worldview. I want every person in sales to think about what I am about to write. You have heard it countless times: You have two ears and one mouth, so you should be *lis-*

> *You have two ears and one mouth, so you should be listening twice as much as you talk.*

tening twice as much as you talk. And quite frankly, we should be talking much less than that. And this is hard— very hard. Most salespersons get by through persistence, follow up, hard work, and an outgoing personality. This is not a bad start. However, we can do so much more. We can go so much further. Are you willing? Good.

I want to really focus on how well we listen. Before we do that, let's pause and define the difference in "hearing" and "listening," as the two words are oftentimes used interchangeably. Hearing is simply the act of perceiving sound by ear. Simply said, as long as you have good hearing, it just happens. We hear many things each day in our constantly connected world. The question is then, how many of these things will we actually remember? In my case, unless I am actively paying attention, I may hear words or noise, but have little recall of what was said as I am in my own world when I am not working (Just ask my wife). Thus, listening is different and requires one to consciously pay attention to what someone is saying. This is where the term *active listening* comes from.

> *One of the greatest needs of a human being is to be listened to and understood.*

Let me give you an easy way to determine if someone has listened to you. Explain to the person whatever it is you want to say. Once you are done, have the person repeat your message back to you. If they are successful in doing so, they have listened; and if they cannot, they have simply been hearing you talk. Most people hear what we say but do not stop and actively listen to what we say. Guess what? One of the greatest needs of a human being is to be listened to and understood. We do not meet this need if we cannot understand what others have told us. If we spend our time talking over them or thinking about what we want to say next, we are not listening and understanding. And again, this is very hard for many of us.

Do we seek to truly understand another person? Do we ask them deep open-ended questions so we can hear what they have to say and make them feel important? Or are we simply pretending and paying as little attention as possible to make it seem like we are actually listening? Are there missed opportunities to build relationships because we do not get to know another person better? In other words, we have talked to them or "at them" a lot, but have learned little about them. We instead have focused on our needs, wants, and desires. I can do better, and I am sure you can as well.

The people I enjoy the most, in all parts of life, are those who are the best listeners. Why? These people make me feel important. Don't we all want to feel that way? So I challenge you like I have challenged myself. Will you work to improve in this area? Will

Such strong listening skills will not only make you a better person, but also a better professional, communicator, and leader in any endeavor of life.

you seek to consistently improve your listening skills? Such strong listening skills will not only make you a better person, but also a better professional, communicator, and leader in any endeavor of life. Oh yeah, and listening is a big part of what makes people want to buy from you as a salesperson.

I have found that when a person can help me uncover an issue or solve a problem I did not know existed, then I am more likely to buy from him or her. So the modern salesperson who has unlimited data at his or her fingertips must talk less and listen more. There are a series of letters we have seen for years as WIFM (What's In It For Me), but the more important concept we need to remember is a new call station; WIFT (What's In It For Them). Sales is all about the other person. You are simply the one sharing the story, solving the other's pain, making their lives easier, and looking for a good fit between the two parties.

The late Stephen Covey discussed the idea of a "talking stick" as a way to get people to understand this concept. Let's expand upon this a little and use a "smart phone" instead. Say I hand you my phone. Until you give it back to me, you have the floor to talk. You explain what it is you are trying to communicate in an uninterrupted manner, and I must listen. I am not allowed to talk while you have the phone. When you are done sharing your message, you ask if I understood what you said. At that time, you give the phone back to me, and I tell you what "my understanding" is of what you said. Often, this will go back and forth several times. By using the smart phone, which is something we quickly become aware of when it is out of our possession, we are reminded to be more active listeners. The exercise does not end until you are satisfied that I have completely listened and understood what you had to say, and I can accurately repeat it back to you.

Let's now focus on the word *stop*. We must slow down and stop so we can be present in the moment. Remember, yesterday is the past, tomorrow is the future, but today is the *present*. Right now I want you to quit anything you're thinking about or doing for a moment and just be still. I want us to think of *stop* in this manner: Close your eyes and visualize a traffic light that is about to turn red. Envision that you

> *Remember, yesterday is the past, tomorrow is the future, but today is the* present.

are in a car that is heading toward the traffic light and needs to slow down. Now envision what could happen if you do not slow down and instead you enter the busy intersection. You feel a sense of danger. Visualize the surroundings, the sights, sounds, and smells as you work to stop your car at the red light up ahead. Can you visualize this? Good. This is the type of word picture I need you to have in your mind when you find yourself not listening to someone. Recall this red stoplight and the feeling of danger if you do not slow down. And then say the word *stop* out loud! This works, my friends. Try it and see.

I have developed an acronym that will help us reflect on the word STOP:

S: *Simple* – keep things basic. Don't make basic things more difficult than they need to be. Block out all unnecessary distractions so you can focus. In other words, put last things last so you focus on what really matters: the person you are listening to.

T: *Time Out* – slow down and breathe. The antidote to this fast-moving (constantly connected) world is the realization that we cannot outrun things, and that there is only so much time in the day. Again, we are human *beings* not human *doings*. So take time and reflect on where you are heading, and make time for who you are with and where you are. Enjoy the present.

O: *Open-minded* – being receptive to new ideas. Are you willing to admit there may be a better way of doing things? Are you open to learning from another person and hearing his or her ideas? Will you take yourself out of the equation when considering a new concept, idea, or suggestion? Will you ask questions to gain another's insights and carefully consider what he/she has to say? Being open-minded to new ways of thinking is vital to sales success.

P: *Persistent* – continual follow through to stay on top of things. Persistence is a special quality where one never gives up. Persistent people push forward in an aggressive manner and try every available possibility to try and "find a way" to make something work. This quality is one where a person never backs up and never backs down (until one sees he or she is at a dead-end). They give 100 percent in all that they do and leave it "all on the field." There is a fine line between being persistent and being a pest. The goal is to be persistent right up to the point of being a pest.

Now that you have these tools, be sure to *stop* and get ready to *listen* to the next chapter. We are about to get to some why level thinking. Hang with me and don't ask me why (just yet).

CHAPTER 6:

Why Ask Why?

The focus of this chapter is why we do what we do, and why others do what they do. In almost every encounter, I see people talking about the "hows" and "whats" which is the surface level, without clearly articulating their "below-the-surface" reasoning of why they feel

If you ask someone a series of below-the-surface why questions, you will get his/her why.

the way they do. So how do we understand another person's "under the iceberg" reasons? It begins with asking great questions. We all desire to be understood. If you ask someone a series of below-the-surface *why* questions, you will get his/her why. What made us stop asking so many questions and being so curious? Some of us were told to quit asking, and over time we simply stopped. The basic question of "why" teaches us, as parents, to better

Asking "why" makes us reach much deeper levels of understanding with others.

communicate with our children, and teaches us, as adults, not to settle for a surface-level answer. As employees or employers, it allows us to get to deep-rooted issues that lie under the surface. And this is one of the most vital skills of your job as a salesperson. Asking "why" makes us reach much deeper levels of understanding with others, but over time many of us have become satisfied with surface-level answers of "hows" and "whats." Why?

When we got to a certain age, we most likely felt as if we should know it all. In other cases, we failed to ask why because we did not want to look dumb. So we just quit digging and stopped asking. One of the biggest problems a salesperson has is failing to ask deep, open-ended questions to clients or prospects. Asking great questions will allow you to learn more by discovering things that are only possible with this deep-level thinking and questioning. Unfortunately, many salespersons talk more than they listen, having instead been taught to be aggressive and to push to close the sale. As covered in my first book, I am not sure anyone likes this type of salesperson. Most salespersons are not just poor listeners, they are also weak in their question-asking skills.

While writing this section of the book, I had lunch with my youngest daughter (who is in second grade) and some of her friends (and, yes, I looked like Will Ferrell in *Elf*). I admired how creative and curious in nature these kids were. They made me laugh, and they were not afraid to ask me questions. You see, the "fear of asking a dumb question" has not gotten to them yet. The people I admire most in our society are continual learners and childlike at heart. These kids reminded me that many of us have forgotten how to ask questions, how to come up with creative ideas, or how to look at things in an unorthodox way. While I was there, they asked me such things as: Why is the universe so big? Why is school food so gross? Why did you come here in the rain? Why do you like football so much? And on it went. They asked and I answered. They listened. They laughed and repeated back to me what I said. I listened then laughed. My daughter was smiling at me and her friends the whole

> *However, something more important than being goal oriented is the concept of being growth oriented.*

time. Kids get it right and use the word "why" naturally. We likely started out right; however, as we get older, we tend to lose sight of our creative and open-minded ways.

Many people are goal oriented, which is a good thing. We should be goal oriented so we can track our progress and seek to improve ourselves. However, something more important than being *goal* oriented is the concept of being *growth* oriented. This means you are a continual learner, that you don't mind "looking dumb" in order to seek a new way of doing things. This is the type of person who is not afraid to "zig" in one direction when everyone else "zags" in another. With only a goal-oriented mindset, you miss or hit your goal and are done. However, with a growth-oriented mindset, there is always more to do, see, learn, and grow. In *Alice in Wonderland*, (my words, not direct quotes) Alice comes to the fork in the road and asks the Cheshire cat which way she should go. The cat asks Alice where she wants to go. Alice says she doesn't know. The Cheshire cat replies, "... then it doesn't matter what road you take."

In life, we are either growing and moving forward, or declining and falling backward.

This is a great example and illustration of the difference in being focused on goals and on growth. A goal, once achieved, always comes to an end like the fork in the road. However, unlike Alice, people who are focused on continual growth know exactly which road they want to take as the journey never stops. In life, we are either growing and moving forward, or declining and falling backward. There is no such thing as staying the same. The only difference in you now and a year from now will be what you have learned, seen, experienced, and thus improved. If you have done none of these things, you will have gone backward.

Have you noticed how we are programmed to ask someone how they are doing when oftentimes, beyond being polite, we really are not that interested? For instance, if a person really wanted to stop and talk to us then and there about a deep issue in his or her life, are we prepared to listen, or are we assuming we would get the normal response, which is, "I'm doing super," or, "I'm doing great." The fact is both could be having a terrible day. This is very much surface-level thinking. Why do both football players and coaches at all levels say they are going to watch film? Why do music artists say they are working on a new record? Note: In case you don't know, the football players and coaches are not watching film, as it is not used anymore, and everything is digital. However, this is what has always been said in football, so it is still said today. And musicians will not be asking you to purchase a record player even though they mentioned their record. Again, this is the jargon that has been passed down in that industry and has thus become the norm of what people say.

Here is another one. NBC did a nice job promoting their show *Peter Pan Live!* that came out in late 2014. I did not see the show so cannot comment on it. However, I want to discuss their thought process from my vantage point. I believe the reason the network promoted this show so heavily (yes, I saw the promotions a lot while watching football) was so people would *actually watch the show live.* Huh? The *old* norm of live shows is now *new*? Yes, and thus it was different. The fact that it was "live," which we see so seldom these days, made us want to watch it and tweet along as if we were watching a Broadway show. So I give NBC a lot of credit as they indeed thought at a deeper level.

In contrast, I did not hear anyone say anything, at least not to me, about this being a *live* show, why it was a live show, or even giving it a second thought. However, if you think deeply for a moment, all television shows used to be broadcast live, and now most are produced well in advance. And as viewers, we DVR our favorite shows and watch them when we please. Did most people take the time to reflect that the network was simply taking an old concept and reintroducing it to a new era? I doubt it. If you think about it, all of these examples, whether buzz words in football, or music, or the old becoming new again, are surface level in nature. We have learned to look at things in an above-the-surface manner and accept them as they are. We don't take time to ask or think about "why," and thus we are not embracing an "under the iceberg mindset." And don't forget this makes up approximately 90% of the iceberg.

> *We have learned to look at things in an above-the-surface manner and accept them as they are.*

To grow in sales, we must be able to fully understand another person's why. The "5 Whys Communications Model," which is covered as an entire chapter in my *Everyone is in Sales* book, helps us get to the root reason. If you ask another person approximately five "why" questions, you will be able to reach the source of the issue (under the iceberg) and gain real information, which in turn will give you results. This method not only helps focus our conversations, but also helps us gain a better understanding of others.

Here is an example that relates to the printing industry I do consulting work in:

Salesperson:Why didn't we get the printing for that brochure job?

Buyer:Your price was too high.

Salesperson:Why was our price higher?

Buyer: Well, I am not sure offhand, but it seemed to be higher based on my quick review of the quotes received.

Salesperson: Why did our quote seem to be higher than the others you received, based on your review?

Buyer:As I remember, you built a lot of additional options into the base price and as "add on" options that the others did not have.

Salesperson:Why was that a bad thing?

Buyer: You know, it was actually quite helpful, and you gave me some great ideas. Now that I think about it, you doing that may have made your price seem high.

Salesperson:Why didn't you compare everything "apples to apples" to ensure accuracy?

Buyer: Honestly, I planned (due to time) to go with my current printer, but now based on what you have told me, I am going to go back and review this in more detail. You have asked me some questions that make me wonder if I am getting the value I thought I was. Perhaps I have somehow overlooked the best option, which may have been you.

Bingo! Five questions (on average) get you to the "root reason" of why someone does what they do. As Covey said, "Seek first to understand then to be understood." This is what this entire chapter is about. If you don't ask enough probing questions to get to a person's why, there is no way you will truly understand them. And if we do not understand others we will never be effective in sales or marketing.

Why ask why means that we must find our inner child and become curious again. Curiosity leads to creativity. One key to being creative is asking those you respect questions to see what has been done before, what has worked, what has not worked, and to find possible new ways of doing things. I personally

> Why ask why *means that we must find our inner child and become curious again.*

have no desire to hit every pothole in the road while driving if someone can let me know in advance where those potholes are. It's the same with life. Why don't we listen more to wise people around us, ask good questions, and then develop the best course of action? Is it pride? Being stubborn? Because you know it all?

Our most advanced learners absorb information from a variety of credible sources and take the time to carefully analyze it. There is no such thing as a stupid *ques-*

tion. However, there is such a thing as a stupid *answer*. If someone is too busy, thinks he or she has seen it all, is too proud to ask questions and learn, then that person is in danger of operating as a "how and what" surface-level person. By the way, these types of people are not in high demand in the workforce. They like to memorize stuff, do things the same way they always have, and enjoy telling stories from the past. The key to an "under the iceberg mindset" can be seen as we examine the taxonomy below. The original taxonomy was created nearly 60 years ago by Dr. Benjamin Bloom, and this revised one was updated in the 1990s. http://www.celt.iastate.edu/teaching-resources/effective-practice/revised-blooms-taxonomy/ It goes from the simplest form of learning, which is surface level, to the most advanced form of learning, which is *under the iceberg.*

- **Remembering:** can the person recall or remember the information?

- **Understanding:** can the person explain the ideas or concepts?

- **Applying**: can the person use the information in a new way?

- **Analyzing**: can the person distinguish between the different parts?

- **Evaluating**: can the person justify a stand or decision?

- **Creating**: can the person create a new product or new point of view?

You can see learning in its simplest form is all about remembering or memorizing things. Some things are good to know, such as multiplication tables. You can simply memorize them, and you are done. As you move down the list, each level gets deeper in learning. I want us to focus on the final one, which is creating. I believe this is the highest level of learning. In my role as a professor, speaker, and consultant, I get to see these different levels a great deal. The "creating learner" is the one who will read this book, understand it, "mine it" for ideas he or she agrees with, will see new possibilities that I didn't cover (How could that happen? Just kidding. I'm just making sure you are with me), and then will take this concept and build it into something new. This person can explain the learned concepts from a different point of view, and in short make the learning his or her own, thus creating something new for others. I always say that people can copy your ideas, but they cannot replicate your DNA. Simply said, they cannot be you. Only you can be you.

> *However, to outthink, lead, market, and sell in 2015 and beyond, requires the highest level of learning.*

Sharing ideas, quoting people, and retweeting others' thoughts are good. Internalizing them and being able to explain them is fine. However, to outthink, lead, market, and sell in 2015 and beyond, requires the highest level of learning. It requires a commitment to continual and lifelong learning. When you can always seek new ideas, possibilities, and angles, and bring them forth in an educated manner, then you are a person who will always be gainfully employed and the best at what you do. Most people are not willing to put enough time into a subject to master it, and thus they never truly advance far enough to make it their own. Consequently, they keep doing the same things over and over and expecting a different result. I hear that this is the definition of insanity.

Albert Einstein stated, "The world as we have created it is a process of our thinking. It cannot be changed without changing our thinking." This means that we must be open to listening to what others have to say and be willing to change our thinking if it is off base.

Aristotle argued, "It is the mark of an educated mind to be able to entertain a thought without accepting it." This means we do not have to believe something that someone says and make it our own truth. We must run it through all the filters and realize that even if we do not agree with something, we should still actively listen to what the person is sharing. Again, we must seek first to understand.

As we come to the end of this chapter, I challenge you to change your thinking. Get rid of the old notion that your job in a presentation is "selling something." Make it your goal to become skilled at asking questions. And remember, you are there to "interview" the buyer to get to their root-level pain source so you can help them feel better. You are sharing your story with them (after asking them questions) to see if there is a fit between what they need and what you can offer.

For example, you could ask them questions such as: If you could change one thing with your current vendor, what would it be and why? Why would you consider making a change? If you had a magic wand and could draw up the perfect supplier, what would that company look like and why?

I hope you see how these deep probing questions are about the buyer and are open ended. Allow them to do the talking until you know what to say based on what they have shared. In sales, there is an opportunity behind every obstacle, and a solution behind every problem. You must not focus on what is wrong in a situation, but instead flip the issue on its head. Remember, most people focus on the problem and not the solution. And your goal is to attack the problem in a new and creative way. This is the difference between people who say "Yes, but," and those who say "Yes, and." The "Yes, but" people acknowledge an idea has promise, yet always find some problem with it. In contrast, the "Yes, and" people see the validity of an idea and add something positive to it that helps to make the idea even better.

> *Remember, most people focus on the problem and not the solution.*

Will you be the one who gets their business? Trust me, they are buying from someone. Will you ask enough good questions and think at a deep enough level so they choose to purchase from you? Thus, dig deeper and actively listen to what a potential buyer says so you can ask the best questions. And, always reflect on this point:

What is it that you want a buyer to feel, to know, or to do once they have heard your offering? Like Covey said, we must "…begin with the end in mind." Remember that an "under the iceberg mindset" begins with "why."

Hang on tight as we move on to Section 3. We will learn how our brand, after taking all we have learned so far into account, makes all the difference in answering the question, "*Would You Buy from You?*"

SECTION III:

Your Brand Makes the Difference

CHAPTER 7:

Everyone Has a Brand

We communicate a message in everything we do, and it's especially true when we use the term "brand." We discuss brands all the time. Why? Because brands stand out in our minds. Think about our instant recognition of Nike's *Just Do It* or Apple's *There's an App for That* campaigns. These messages effectively connect customers with the brand. The goal is to make such a brand experience personal in nature. For example, are you a McDonald's or Burger King person? Is it Coke or Pepsi? Do you prefer a Mac or PC? You get the idea.

So what is a brand? It is *not* (as people often think) a logo or product/service. Yes, a logo is what we see, and a product or service is what we purchase. But those are facts and features. A brand is alive and further develops

89

in some manner each day. It is the "gut feeling" we have when we think about a person or an organization. A brand is the sum total of key ideas, emotions, and perceptions that are communicated to your audience and associated with you and/or your organization's work. When your stakeholders reflect upon their experiences with you or your organization, the brand is the "shorthand" way of summing up those characteristics and feelings.

A brand is the sum total of key ideas, emotions, and perceptions that are communicated to your audience and associated with you and/or your organization's work.

To help simplify this subject, I have developed an updated acronym for BRAND: the *Baseline* (a minimum or starting point used for comparisons) reading of one's *Reputation, Attributes, Name,* and *Distinctiveness. Reputation* is all you stand for; *Attributes* are the characteristics others use when describing you; your *Name* suggests something (good, bad, or indifferent) when a person hears it; and your *Distinctiveness* answers the query, "Why you? What makes you different or unique?" So the question is not if we have a brand (or not)—because we do. All individuals have a brand. All organizations have a brand. Rather, the question is: What do we do with our brand? Jeff Bezos, founder of Amazon, said, "Your brand is what people say about you when you're not in the room." I agree Mr. Bezos.

Our brand is not defined by what *we* say it is, but is characterized by what *others* say it is. To that end, successful individuals and organizations work hard to develop their brands through effective communications. Always remember that building a strong, recognizable, and consistent brand takes time, effort, and commitment. It requires a deliberate, purposeful, and intentional sales and marketing strategy. However, our brand, as it is more difficult to measure on a financial report, is oftentimes overlooked. Strong brand loyalty is one of the most valuable assets any individual or organization can have. Quite frankly, strong brand loyalty explains why customers will pay more for our goods and services. This is what I call *value*, and it is much different than the price of your offerings. Your price is your price. If your business model is to be the lowest price, you better find a way to keep lowering your price, as there is always a competitor who will undercut you, and who will either duplicate

> *Strong brand loyalty is one of the most valuable assets any individual or organization can have.*

what you offer or try to improve upon it. However, there is only so much cutting any company can do. So, I don't recommend low pricing as a branding strategy unless you have the global buying power and clout of a company like Walmart.

Let's focus, then, on our brand being one that is built on value. Here is my definition of value. Value = Price + Goods/Services + *You*. Do you see that *You* are a key part of the equation that makes up value? (The book title is starting to make sense huh?) If you do not bring anything to the table, then you are simply a price. Value is indeed one main answer to the question *Would You Buy from You?* Remember, your brand is that "extra value" you provide and the reason a customer continually chooses you over similar competitors or offerings in the market. When you are seen as the best in the niche business you focus on, then price is not the issue. People will pay more for a brand that they respect and feel there is no substitute for.

When pondering your brand, you must first determine what it is all about. What do you want people to say, feel, and remember about you and your company distinctly? Remember, your brand is not what *you* say it is, but what *others* say it is. So, you should obtain feedback from those around you as a first step. Be sure to obtain this 360-degree feedback from those close and those more removed from you. In other words, you need a diverse group of individuals who will provide objective feedback. Once you know what your brand is, you can determine the ways you want to purposefully grow, change, re-frame, promote, and/or strengthen your current brand position. And remember, this uniqueness is a living organism. So, how do you define your brand? Does it matter? You bet it does.

> *So, how do you define your brand? Does it matter? You bet it does.*

My colleague, Ted Rubin, a global marketing expert, shared his thoughts on branding with me. "Big business and celebrities place a great deal of emphasis on developing, exuding, and promoting their brand," he said. "I agree strongly with you, Ryan, that this concept should be applied by everyone seeking to differentiate themselves in today's personal and business worlds. Granted, large brands have cash to throw at social campaigns and advertising—but the lesson on developing personality can be adopted by anyone, large or small. And that's more important than ever these days, because the online arena is getting more and more crowded. Even if you're a one-person band, you need to be thinking about developing a unique online personality, something that separates you from your competitors and helps you stand out. So how can the little guy develop personality? Well, maybe you have a passion for collecting something that you can tie in. My quirky personality thing is fun socks—the louder and crazier the better. I take pictures of my sock-clad feet when I'm traveling and post them—it's something I've become known for over time. It's a fun part of my personal brand that strikes a chord with many of my business relationships, friends, and followers. I post them to all my social channels and have a Pinterest board... We Heart Socks. The important thing is to understand is that whatever you do in social channels, it should be genuine and a natural fit for who you are as a person. So start thinking of ways that you can involve your social audiences in something that's uniquely you—something that will encourage them to want to interact with you and get to know you better. Passing your audience's 'personality test' is often a good way to get a foot in the door that leads to developing that all-important Return on Relationship... *#RonR!*" Folks, Ted nailed it.

> *Remember, only you can be you, and this wonderful thing should be used to your utmost advantage in growing your brand.*

I want to focus on two concepts he mentioned. The first is "be uniquely you" and the second is the power of "relationships." We must embrace who we are and communicate it in a consistent manner through all of our channels (online and offline) to grow our brand. Remember, *only you can be you, and this wonderful thing should be used to your utmost advantage in growing your brand.* Also, it is vital that we never forget that all of our sales, communication efforts, and marketing strategies center around (if done right) growing human relationships. There is no magic trick

> *We all have a unique imprint, and thus, we must focus on what we do with it.*

or shortcut to doing this. It takes a methodical, genuine, and consistent dedication to being truly helpful to others without expecting something in return. And we need to remind ourselves "why" we are doing what we are doing (reflect on your "why" level thinking in Section 2).

We all have a unique imprint, and thus, we must focus on what we do with it. If you take Ted's example about socks, you can see that anything, if done in an original, fun, and caring manner, can be a differentiator for you. This applies to an individual as much as it does to an organization. The same principles apply to both. We pre-

94

fer to buy from people who are real, who we believe in, and, most importantly, who we trust. My colleague Kim Garst, branding expert and author, said, "God made us all unique! We all have unique ways of expressing ourselves and, if you will just be *you*, you will be astonished at how that builds a brand that will attract the right customers and clients! Frankly, there is nothing new under the sun. It's all been done before in some fashion but it's how each individual shows up and makes that concept their own. That's what attracts the right people to your brand!"

I completely agree with this. And it is not only my or Kim's opinion. We have been created by God in His image, and we are all unique creations. Luke 12:7 (NIV) says, "Indeed, the very hairs of your head are all numbered. Don't be afraid; you are worth more than many sparrows." The fact that we are so deeply loved and valued by God is difficult to comprehend. I have a hard time grasping this concept as I fail so often. However, I am extremely thankful. It is comforting to realize God already knows everything about us and made us the way we are with our own DNA and distinct personality. Nobody else can be you. Nobody else could be me (I know a lot of you are saying *thank goodness*). However, this does not mean we cannot grow, change, improve, etc. Life is all about the process of doing this. Thus, we have a brand that begins developing when we are born and grows in some manner throughout our life. And remember, an organization is simply a formal structure that consists of individuals. It, too, grows and changes.

I would be remiss not to share how brands can easily get lost in our constantly connected world (discussed in Section 1). Here is an example of a brand being overlooked. Have you noticed that when a car alarm goes off these days, nobody pays attention? In contrast, 15 years ago we would have stopped everything we were doing to see what was going on, assuming someone was breaking into a car. Why do I bring this up? The distraction of the car alarm mirrors the noise that takes place all around us. And when we get too accustomed to seeing something, we tune it out and no longer pay any attention to it. If we are not careful in how we consistently build our brand across all channels—including the biggest one, which is in person—then it is in jeopardy of being lost in the noise. Picture a restaurant. Music is playing, televisions are on, info is scrolling across the TV screens, people are laughing, phones are ringing, texts are beeping, babies are crying, and people are tweeting. There is noise everywhere, and we hardly notice it.

When we get too accustomed to seeing something, we tune it out and no longer pay any attention to it.

Because our message matters, our sales efforts via phone, email, text, in person, and/or via social media are more important than ever. If we do not influence people in a creatively authentic way and successfully break through the turbulence around us, we stand the chance of being overlooked. So let me ask you some questions. Is your sales message unique? Do you provide great sales information and content? Are you creative, consistent, and credible in your sales approach? What are you bringing to people that causes them to want to pay attention? Do you know? If not, you must think about this.

In Section 2 we discussed the importance of understanding both your and others' *why*. However, in this chapter we take it a step further. We must learn to communicate

> *We must learn to communicate in a manner that inspires people.*

in a manner that inspires people. This means we must go beyond sharing facts and figures. We go deeper than the features and benefits we can offer. Thus we must know our own *why* and convey it through our brand. What is our purpose? What do we value? Any person or company can show you services, offerings, and features. However, I do not find that (by itself) inspiring, and most others do not as well. When I ask someone what their company does best, I often hear one or more of these things. "Ryan, we offer great customer service, competitive pricing, top quality work, one-stop shopping, unparalleled talent, a rich history, and many years in business, plus we are an industry leader." Huh? Everyone says this stuff. It does not cause me to want to be a part of something. In fact, these are just buzzwords that do not get to *why*. This is the difference between a one-time sales *transaction* and an ongoing sales *interaction*.

Picture it this way. In a *transaction* you are sitting across the table from someone as a customer vs. vendor. However, in a sales *interaction*, you are sitting at the table beside someone as customer and buyer partners. So, when you hear someone say all the buzzwords of why they are great, (and they all sound the same) what do you do? You go with whom you trust (This will be covered in detail in Chapter 9). If people know what your cause or belief is and what your *why* is, they will see value in you if they share the same beliefs and vision. This is why some people make decisions with their gut or heart. It feels like the right decision because you trust someone. The buyer can see what all the numbers, facts, and features say, but something does not feel right. It is your heart that a brand (done well) appeals to. We pay more to buy Nike apparel and goods because we believe (at some level) their products will help us perform better if we are wearing them. We do not see it as a cost, but as an investment. And Nike has built a brilliant brand. A friend became "gung ho" about jogging a couple years ago. I must say I was proud of her dedication. However, when I saw her jogging a few months later, decked out in all new Nike gear, I could not resist saying something. I told her, "You know, with your new Nike wardrobe, you should easily be able to take a couple minutes off your 5K time." True story, and an example of the power of a brand in action.

Here is my challenge to you as we close this chapter. When considering your company as the best choice for a customer, answer the following in 12-17 seconds or less: "Who are you? What do you do? Why does it matter?" We are all pretty good at answering the first two since these are "how and what" level questions. However, most of us struggle in answering the third question of "who cares" or "why does it matter." Oh yeah, one more thing. You cannot mention (as your reasons) good price, service, or quality as differentiating characteristics. These three are "givens" of any legitimate competitor. BEEP, BEEP, BEEP... there goes the car alarm!

CHAPTER 8:

So What, Why You, Who Cares?

How is that for a chapter title? What do I mean by "So what? Why you? Who cares?" My objective is to change the way we think. As mentioned before, this means that we move from being *goal oriented* (good) to being *growth oriented* (great). Goal setting is important. And I strongly suggest you set such goals (SMART ones) in the various areas of your life. As a reminder, SMART stand for: *Specific, Measurable, Attainable, Relevant, Time-bound.*

Let me give you an example. If you tell me that your goal is, "to sell more this year than last year," is this a SMART goal? No, it is not. However, if you shared with me that your goal is to increase your sales 10 percent in calendar year 2015 over calendar year 2014, this is indeed a SMART goal. As you know, upon achieving a goal,

101

we feel a nice sense of accomplishment. But then, we begin to think about what we will do next (I am begin-ning to feel this way as the writing of this book is near-ing completion). If one goal ends, we need to set another one, right? Thus, my concept is to be growth oriented as growth never stops since we are continually moving

Thus, my concept is to be growth oriented as growth never stops since we are continually moving forward.

forward. When I teach university classes for working adults, I often grade student assignments and add KPF (Keep Pushing Forward) at the end of them. I want stu-dents to remember *why* they are there and to never be-come satisfied with "just getting by." When I was growing up, I had a wise person (older than me) tell me I had two choices as a talented young person. I could either be a "get-by guy" or "get-it-done" guy. I took that message to heart, chose the latter, and haven't taken my foot off the accelerator since.

It is easy to become complacent. Many of us are stuck in the past and talk about the glory days. Some people have lost track of their own growth and live through their children to such a degree that it is difficult to watch. They have somehow gotten their own growth confused with their child's growth. However, the driven people in life like the best salespersons are never satisfied with where they currently are, and always seek ways to im-prove. They always desire to get better. Often the top per-formers are the ones most dedicated to growing more;

whereas the average salespersons—who really need to grow—are "blind" to this need and keep doing things the way they always have, refusing to stretch in new ways. A person's "blind spot" is something he or she is not aware of, but everyone else is. The way to improve is to recognize your blind spot, embrace it, and work on it.

Again, when we are *only* goal oriented, we achieve a goal and are left with that "empty feeling" with regard to what to do next. In contrast, when we are continually growth oriented, we never fully arrive, and instead see life (in each area) as a series of goals—one after another. We know we are a work in progress. When one is growth oriented, that person is committed to continual learning. And if you are not a continual learner, I encourage you to start being one today. Continual learners approach life with an "as if" mindset. This means they think "as if" they could do it today. They are open minded to new ways of doing things. They can answer this question: "2015 will have been a success if _____;" or "2016 will be deemed a success if _____." If you do not know the answer, take a few moments and think about it. Then write it down. How will you know what road you are on or where you are going if you don't consider this?

Let's look at what I call the "blank sheet of paper" approach as a salesperson. Your paper is blank and yours to do with as you please. You have choices about what to do with your paper. You can do nothing and leave it blank (which is not good), or you can bring your creative approach to the equation (which is good) and/or add your unique fingerprint to it (which is very good).

You thus bring your uniqueness to the blank sheet of paper, causing you to look at the sheet differently than everyone else. I call this *zig-zag sales*. You can never be afraid to *zig* even if everyone else chooses to *zag*. After all, they may be wrong. In sales, you must lead, follow, or get out of the way. Sometimes

> *You can never be afraid to* zig *even if everyone else chooses to* zag.

this means you must zig and take the road less traveled. And guess what? Sometimes you will look really smart, and others will follow your lead. Other times you will be wrong, and others will smirk or laugh at you. However, you swung the bat and tried. Our character in life is developed by trying to improve.

When I began my career in sales, I saw everything as wide open. Veteran salespersons would tell me, "Ryan, that is a waste of time," or, "Your idea will never work." I was not deterred. In time I proved many of them wrong. You see, I was determined to outwork, outthink, out-learn, and outperform the competition with a focus on continual learning and growth. I knew success would not happen overnight, but I was focused on the long-haul, with goals as check points along the way. And I have never stopped. What about you? There is no better time than now to change your mindset from the old *think outside the box* saying to the one I call *break the box*. This means you are no longer confined by a *box* or any old way of thinking. People like this are special, and, yes, they are the ones people buy from. Good salespersons can overcome an objection. Great salespersons can anticipate an objection before it comes up. This is a big difference, and it comes down to being the best you can be (growth oriented) and never becoming complacent with "I know it all" or "I have seen it all." We can all learn something new each and every day. My youngest daughter must have heard the word *box* too much as she recently asked my wife, "Mom, can we think inside the box for a moment?" She has learned something new as well, and she is not even eight.

> *Good salespersons can overcome an objection. Great salespersons can anticipate an objection before it comes up.*

To effectively answer the chapter's title, "So What? Why You? Who Cares?" we need to consider if we are focused on the right things. Are we doing things the best way? Are we doing them for the right reasons? We need to look at what we should put on our *start doing* list and what needs to go on our *stop doing* list so we can spend our time (168 hours a week, 24/7) as wisely as possible. And we must be prepared to convey value in all that we say and do.

> *We need to look at what we should put on our start doing list and what needs to go on our stop doing list.*

Let's assume you are on a sales call with a prospective client. The prospect says "so what" in regard to your claim that your organization has been in business since 1948—because being in business a long time (by itself) means absolutely nothing. Are the same people employed there? Does the same person answer the phone? You get the idea. However, if you reframe this to the "why" level and explain how you have a third-generation business that has grown in each decade of existence, then you are on the right track. Then you can share that your company's longevity has allowed it to continually invest both externally back to the local community and internally to further develop your staff. Now we have begun to create value. Next, you can discuss that this length of time in business has allowed you to be debt free, thus indicating that you are in a good cash position and not hamstrung by the bank, and that each generation of ownership has grown the company more than the one that proceeded it. With these examples, a potential client can see why being in business since 1948 matters, especially since you would be bringing this same level of dedication and innovation to his or her business. You see, we appreciate our past, are dedicated to the present, and have a clear vision for the future. We are committed to growing with you for many years ahead. This is an entirely different response; one that illustrates *why* those 67 years mean a great deal.

Or maybe a buyer asks "Why you" are the best choice of all the options they have. "*Why* should we choose your organization over the vast amount of other options that we have?" They are really asking if you have created such a compelling, creative, and valuable offering that makes you the only viable choice for them. If your answer is that "you and your firm work quickly and rarely make a mistake," most buyers will not believe this (it sounds like a sales robot). Instead, you must clearly explain your DSF (Differentiating Sales Factor) and the uniqueness that *you* (and *only you*) bring to them. To overcome "So what? Why you? Who cares?" you must have a powerful value proposition that conveys clear and distinct value in the eye of the beholder.

> *You must have a powerful value proposition that conveys clear and distinct value in the eye of the beholder.*

You must articulate your value in solving problems when they arise, and how you find solutions, letting them know how you will handle these things "when they happen." You need to share how you are committed to making their life easier, to reducing their stress and workload, so you can truly become a partner with them instead of being an "order taker." You need to explain how you are invested in them, their company, and their industry, and that you will stop at nothing to help them look good, to give them more time, to give them peace of mind, and to deliver headache relief. Trust me, this is not what they hear from the "typical" salesperson. And if they do hear something like this, it is likely "scripted and unauthentic" in nature. So, "Why you" becomes "How can it *not* be you?"

The final question is "Who cares?" Our response must demonstrate how our individual brand or distinctive identity makes the difference. The buyers want to know what's in it for them. Are you seen as a cost or an investment? A partner or a vendor? A one-time transaction (short-term) or a series of ongoing (long-term) interactions? You must explain how you specialize in their industry, understand it, and continually study it to keep abreast of what is going on. You share that you look at what their competition does as well as what their customers are saying. You follow them through digital media channels so you are in on the conversation. And thus you are seen as an extension of your client's team. You are their "eyes and ears." You sit next to them at the table (partner) versus sitting across from them at the table (vendor). You convey your value and demonstrate all the extra things you bring to the equation. Thus, in turn, your price is just a small part of their reason for their ultimate decision to buy from you. Is price a factor in the decision? In most cases it is. However, it is just one part since the greater your value, the less of a factor price plays in the buying decision. So yes, Mr. and Mrs. Salesperson, even in 2015 most people want to purchase value, but only if they can see it. If you cannot convey the value you can bring to them, then they will have a "Who cares" attitude and will do business with the least expensive party.

> *Your goal then is to define the moment and not let the moment define you.*

Since their perception of you is their reality in regard to what you are saying, your goal then is to define the moment and not let the moment define you. You must proactively create the reality you want others to see in your brand. Step by step. Medium by medium. Day by day. Methodically, authentically, and consistently. Thus, you

108

must articulate your unique brand through each communication medium you use. And let me share something with you: There is no such thing as a "secret sauce" that you have or your company has. The only unique thing we have… (drum roll)…is *you*.

My colleague, Jay Baer, best-selling author and marketing guru, posted a blog on this topic. I asked Jay a few follow up questions for this book and he said, "All businesspeople…fall prey to the curse of the 'secret sauce;' the belief that they possess insights, process, or know-how that is theirs and theirs alone. Often, businesspeople will limit the scope and scale of their content marketing and overall information provision because they are afraid to reveal the secret sauce. There are several problems with that psychology. First, it is unlikely that whatever sauce you have at your disposal is actually a secret. The reality is that 'secret sauce' is usually 'how we've chosen to do things.' Second, whatever theorems and processes the company has adopted are probably already known (or knowable) to competitors. If the company has ever had an employee who has left to join a competitor, the 'secret sauce' is fully understood by that competitor by now. If the company has ever had a customer who has subsequently worked with a competitor, the 'secret sauce' is understood by that competitor by now. The truth is that a list of ingredients doesn't make someone a chef. Even if all the components of the process are given away for free, it doesn't mean that the process itself can be easily replicated. At my consulting firm, Convince & Convert, we routinely publish detailed presentations of how we do social media strategic plans and content marketing strategic plans for major brands. Do competitors download those materials and use them to inform their own work? Probably. But that certainly doesn't invalidate our expertise and experience in stitching it all together successfully for corporate clients. The goal of content marketing is to give away everything you know, but do so one piece at a time. Provide free information snacks that create interest in your knowledge meals."

Jay went on to say, "Many companies are afraid they will not get hired for a project if they have given their info away. And any company who wants to take the ideas from a webinar or PowerPoint and try to do it themselves… to save a few bucks is not the kind of client you want anyway."

Jay, you nailed it out of the park. And, I could not agree more. It is funny how this topic came to life as I was writing this section of the book. I was in the midst of presenting a national webinar series (during this section of the book as well). I gave away my best and total information to the attendees. Upon the conclusion of the series, I offered a complimentary consultation for each company. I saw that even though they had my Power-Point slides, and my recorded webinars, they did not have the

People can copy your ideas, and duplicate your slides, but they cannot replicate you. So, the "secret sauce" (and it is not all that secret) is you!

real thing: *Me.* Thus, I had given them my "secret sauce"

in full, but they wanted *me*. They saw my value. Most attendees signed up for the follow-up consultation. Again, people can copy your ideas, and duplicate your slides, but they cannot replicate you. So, the "secret sauce" (and it is not all that secret) is *you*!

When I began sending in manuscript overviews to publishers for my first book *Everyone is in Sales,* this line of questions became real to me. Publishers get bombarded with book concepts and only want to discuss the best ideas that are well developed. One particular executive helped me a lot by saying my book concept of "everyone is in sales" was good overall. But (and I saw it coming) the person challenged me and said something like, "So what? Everyone is in sales? What does that mean? Why are you the most qualified person to write this book? What makes you believe you can write a book on this topic better than someone else? And, who cares? Who is this book even written to? Is it targeted to everyone? Salespersons? A book targeted to everyone is a book that is written for no one."

You get the idea. This wise person asked me some hard questions. And I did not have any answers. I had to reflect on what I wanted to do, why I was the person to write this book, and who I wanted to target. Ultimately, the book accomplished these goals. However, this line of questioning has stuck with me ever since, and I have asked the "So what? Why you? Who cares?" question to countless groups around the country. It fits in along the same lines as this book's title, *Would You Buy from You?*

In helping salespersons overcome these questions, I often remind them that content is king. And you know what? This isn't quite right. Why? Content is good, but *great* content is "king." In time this may not be enough. Mark Schaefer shared with me, "There is a common saying among… marketers that 'content is king.' That is not true anymore. Great content is only the starting line to enter the race. That is the minimum requirement if you even hope to compete. Instead, we need to turn our attention to ignition, as I describe in detail in my book *The Content Code.* Great content does nothing for a business if it doesn't move, if it is not shared and viewed by customers. Simply creating content that sits on a website is a waste of time and money if it doesn't ignite." So, for now, I will stay with *content is king*, but I see Mark's point and soon *great content* may not be enough to differentiate you. Instead it may become the minimum requirement to get you into the sales or marketing game.

Why do you become engrossed in a movie or TV show? Why do you send a funny video to a friend? Why do you enjoy talking to certain people? Why do you like to read certain articles? The answer is simple. We do these things because we love watching, hearing, or reading creative information or ideas. Everyone is busy. Whether we are in person (offline) or digital (online), it takes something

> *Whether we are in person (offline) or digital (online), it takes something special and unique to pull us in and "wow" us.*

112

special and unique to pull us in and "wow" us. We live in a world where most people have the attention span of a goldfish. So, how does something attract attention? The secret is simple. It is all about doing something remarkable (worthy of making a remark about). With that in mind, I am going to attempt to show you what I mean.

The next time someone *flies off the handle* at you to try to put you *between a rock and a hard place*, consider his or her reasoning. If your goal is to be *clicking on all cylinders*, do not settle for being stuck in a *Catch-22* situation or be limited by *flavor-of-the-month*-type thinking. Instead, work through all the *smoke and mirrors* to ensure that everyone is *on the same page*. What does this mean? Simple: *Cut to the chase* and *get to the bottom line*. Most organizations seek to *raise the bar* in performance so they can get their *foot in the door* with new clients. However, be careful not to *jump the gun* in doing this or you will be *going off half-cocked*. If you move too quickly, *shoot and then aim*, you will get *close, but no cigar*. Then you will be *back to the drawing board*, experiencing a hard fall from *cloud nine*.

Wow! How many of these expressions do we hear all the time? Answer: Many of them. What is so intriguing (hopefully) about my writing them all in one place? First, is it creative to try to put all of these expressions together in an original manner to make a point? Yes. Does it provide intriguing content? Yes. Therefore, in order for a book chapter to be engaging, it must provide more than my wording and your reading. It must be a two-way dialogue not a one-way monologue. It must be about tak-

People can duplicate your information, but they can't replicate your unique genetic code.

ing and processing the words that are in the book (or on the device you are reading from)— words transformed into a story worth sharing and acting upon. Isn't this what you want your customers to do when they think of you? If you sound like everyone else, you lack great content. Always remember: people can duplicate your information, but they can't replicate your unique genetic code. Again, they cannot be you. So the answer to "So what? Why you? Who cares?" is provide creative information in a consistent manner, and then be yourself.

CHAPTER 9:

Develop a PACT: The Intersection of Sales and Marketing

We are nearing the end of this book. Hang with me as we are almost there. Between this chapter and the conclusion we will tie the entire concept of *Would You Buy from You?* together. For years, the roles of sales and marketing have been divided. Marketing's role is to create brand recognition so salespersons can follow their lead and achieve more sales success. Thus, marketing's job, like an offensive coordinator in football, is to call the plays and develop the plan that sales is to follow. The salesperson, like the player, is supposed to execute these marketing plans "on the field." The problem is that most quality marketing persons and talented salespersons do not see things the same way. Based on feedback I have obtained, marketing people feel that the salespersons have more tools (created by marketing) than they could

115

ever use, and they see no reason why the salespersons are not producing at a higher level. In contrast, salespersons view marketing persons as being clueless to what it is like to actually be in sales. They see marketing people coming up with all types of theoretical "ideas and plans," but, view these plans as ones that don't actually work in the field. Let me say that both the sales and marketing professionals are correct. They are each focused on different parts of the pie and often do not understand or appreciate what it is like to be in the other person's shoes.

I have had the unique privilege of overseeing both sales and marketing in a medium-size company and have overseen both functions (of organizations) while consulting. I had to review both segments equally, so I know firsthand how they are different and unique. Marketing has always existed to help sales perform better, and the purpose of the sales team has always been to execute the marketing strategy. There was no finger pointing under my watch as I ensured everyone was on the same page and valued the other. When sales and marketing are working in tandem, the best possible results occur. However, in many organizations, there is a lack of trust or understanding that occurs between the two, resulting in a lot of wasted time and finger pointing.

When sales and marketing are working in tandem, the best possible results occur.

In 2015 and going forward the rules have changed. *Sales and marketing* is a phrase that is often heard (in tandem) but seldom explained. I discussed how the two are different; however, for many, sales and marketing are lumped together and often considered to be the same thing. As an example, many of the educational seminars I attend and speak at have a *Sales and Marketing* track. Moreover, many job titles say *Sales and Marketing Manager* or *VP of Sales and Marketing.* Yes, they are listed together as if they are the same thing. Are they interconnected?

> *We have arrived at the moment in our global world where the* intersection of sales and marketing *must occur.*

Yes. Do they play off of each other? Yes. Are they the same? No. However, we have arrived at the moment in our global world where the *intersection of sales and marketing* must occur. An intersection is defined by dictionary.com, as "a place where two or more roads meet." Sales and marketing can be considered two such roads. Marketing is defined by the Merriam-Webster dictionary as "the activities that are involved in making people aware of a company's products, making sure that the products are available to be bought, etc." In contrast, sales, as defined by freedictionary.com, is the "exchange of goods or services for an amount of money or its equivalent."

So what does this mean and why does this matter? As I stated in my book, *Everyone Is in Sales*, sales is a two-way communications (plural) process. It is where an active conversation between seller and buyer occurs and meets the needs of both parties. It is the actual transaction point where goods, services, and products are purchased. Marketing is about setting up the sale. It focuses on the traditional 4 P's of Marketing (Product, Price, Place, and Promotion).

Today's world demands a multi-faceted, integrated communications approach to reach buyers where they are. So, let's make it easy. In today's world, a salesperson must think like a marketer. He or she must do research, position oneself as an expert, brand him or herself, and provide the best content available to the buyer. A modern marketing professional must think like

> *Salespersons must understand marketing and* market *themselves in their sales efforts. And marketing professionals must be actively* selling.

a salesperson who is presenting (in the field) or making the first contact in prospecting.

So what do we do? We must integrate the two schools of thought. Salespersons must understand marketing and *market* themselves in their sales efforts. And marketing professionals must be actively *selling*, so they must spend time in front of clients, gaining a firsthand experience of what they like, want, and need. Thus we arrive at the intersection of (the roads) sales and marketing. And at this intersection is a street named *brand.* Yes, *Brand* Street. The two disciplines intersect so the customer gets a seamless brand experience that is second to none. Remember, our brand *makes the difference* in answering the question *Would You Buy from You?* It is thus vital to approach all prospect and client opportunities with this integrated approach.

Let's look at ways we must market our brand (the intersection of sales and marketing) to be as effective as possible. To do this I have created six "I" words that must be analyzed so we can answer *Would You Buy from You?* And what letter could be better that *I* in an iPhone, iPod, and iPad world. Here are the *6 I's of Branding*:

1. **Incredible:** What do you bring to the table that is amazing? What do you do that makes people stop, pay attention, and remember what you said so it can be shared with others? What do you do that is remarkable? What do you provide that is extraordinary? If you recall from Section 1, our world is constantly connected; thus, in order to break through the noise and differentiate our brand, we must be incredible in what we say and do. Anything that is incredible is something that will stand out no matter how busy our world is.

2. **Intentional:** Are we purposeful and deliberate in all that we do with our brand? Do we work diligently to keep it consistent throughout all mediums and to take the time needed to ensure consistency? Whether we are talking to someone in person, texting them, or posting something on a social network, it is essential that we are intentional in our approach. We must consciously think through what we are saying/sharing in one area of our life and ensure that it matches up with the other areas of our life. We should always protect our brand carefully. And anything we do, say, share, or write should be

carefully considered so that it fits with our (authentic) brand.

3. **Informative:** What type of information are you sharing with prospects and clients? We discussed content before, but I will say it again. The high level of content that is expected of you, as a salesperson who now thinks as a marketer, is unprecedented. Do you provide information that helps your customer sleep easier? Do you share ideas that they have not had time to think about? The information you share should

> *The high level of content that is expected of you, as a salesperson who now thinks as a marketer, is unprecedented.*

be educational in nature and should save your customers time from having to find it themselves. Your content should be enlightening so that traditional concepts can be viewed in new ways. Is the information you share of value? Is it relevant to what they are struggling with and need answers to? You must provide helpful and timely information on a regular basis to be deemed informative.

4. **Integrity:** A brand cannot be strong if it's not built with integrity. Your brand can only make the difference if it is built upon ethics, honesty, and trust. Anything less is a shortcut (gimmick, trick, etc.) that will not stand the test of time. A brand's integrity is human. It is real and transparent. It does not try to be something it is not. A brand built with integrity is genuine and reflects strong moral principles. Integrity can be seen in how we con-

duct ourselves day in and day out. Do we walk the talk? If so, then we have a brand built with integrity.

5. Inspirational. Does your brand inspire others? Do you motivate them to stretch beyond what is comfortable? We'll take a quick time-out for an example. Stretch your arm up toward the ceiling as high as you can. Good job. Now,

> *When you inspire others, they do something because they want to, not because they have to.*

(now yelling as loud as you can) *REALLY STRETCH!* Did you notice your arm went up a few more inches? You thought you were pushing hard, but you were able to stretch even farther when you were inspired (or scared) into doing so. When you inspire others, they do something because they want to, not because they have to. There is a big difference between the two. A former pastor and friend of mine told me that if I could get people to volunteer, embrace, and help the recreation ministry I was trying to start at the church (without pay), then I had truly inspired them to action. And if I could not, I had not inspired people the right way. The people did come onboard, and he was right. When people buy into a cause greater than themselves, they do so because they are inspired. Thus, inspiration is a key component of our brand.

6. Innovative: Do you hear sayings like *think outside the box* and cringe? Do you instead wish someone would say *go away box* or *smash the box* or something else that is not the same old thing? An innovative person

121

tries to take any obstacle and turn it into an opportunity. He or she seeks to take any problem and find a solution. I was reading the biography of Steve Jobs not long after he passed away, and an example of innovation came to mind. If you can recall when all the free music downloads were going on, with Napster and others, where people burned their music on CDs, this will help. Apple's engineers tried to convince Jobs to change the way the CD door of the Mac computer looked and worked. The way it was designed at that time did not allow for Mac users to download free music. However, Jobs would not budge as he did not like the way the computer would look with a reengineered CD drawer. His staff felt defeated. However, innovation was at work. Steve Jobs was working on something bigger and better. This circumstance ultimately led to the invention of digital music that we now refer to as *iTunes*.

Being innovative creates great value, and I challenge you to make this a key part of your brand. With that said, you should now have a good feel for what a brand is after reading this section of the book and our focus on the *6 I's of Branding*. However, one thing is left to be done. And that is to answer the question *Would You Buy from You?* I have alluded to reasons people would buy from you many times, but now is the time to give you some final takeaways.

Consider the word PACT as being the answer to this book's question. Merriam Webster defines a pact as "a formal agreement between two people or groups." Focus on the word "agreement." Now let's use this to answer,

"Would You Buy from You?" The short answer is a seller and buyer must develop a PACT (*Passion, Authenticity, Creativity* and *Trust*). One person buys from another person when they can "feel" *authentic passion* fueled with *creativity* that is built on *trust.*

The first term in our acronym is *Passion.* Jon Bon Jovi stated, "Nothing is as important as passion. No matter what you want to do with your life, be passionate." This is so true. Steve Jobs said this, "You

> *One person buys from another person when they can "feel" authentic passion fueled with creativity that is built on trust.*

have to be burning with an idea, or a problem, or a wrong that you want to right. If you're not passionate enough from the start, you'll never stick it out." And Jobs nailed it. Without a high level of passion, people bail out when things get difficult. So let me ask you, is your passion contagious? Is it full of energy and enthusiasm? Is it attractive in a way that others cannot resist? Does it move people to take action? Such passion makes other people want to get involved or purchase something as they

> *Without a high level of passion, people bail out when things get difficult.*

are "emotionally moved" by your high level of passion.

The second component of PACT is *Authenticity.* This means you are real and genuine—and conduct yourself the same in all aspects of your life. Thus, you are consistent in behavior. This includes times when you mess

Authenticity is about doing what is right no matter who is or is not watching.

up. Authentic people are the real deal and are both truthful and transparent. Hubert Humphrey said, "Just be what you are and speak from your guts and heart—it's all a man has." And Humphrey is right. All we have is how we live our life, our reputation, and our word. Authenticity is about doing what is right no matter who is or is not watching. Mother Theresa said, "Honesty and transparency make you vulnerable. Be honest and transparent anyway." Wow. What an awesome statement. Authenticity is not about being perfect. It is being true to yourself in spite of what your circumstances are. I don't know about you, but I love spending time with authentic people. So this is a key quality of the PACT that salespersons must exude.

The third component of PACT is Creativity. You can be passionate and authentic, but unless your approach is creative, I may not choose to buy from you. Why? It may be simply because you did not catch my attention or your message never came through the noise. Thomas Edison said, "There's a way to do it better—find it." Since he was so creative, we would be wise to heed his advice. Walt Disney, one of the most creative people I have ever studied, said, "Around here,

There is no bypassing creativity as a salesperson. It is an essential requirement now and in the years ahead.

we don't look backwards for very long. We keep moving forward, opening up new doors and doing new things, because we're curious...and curiosity keeps leading us down new paths." If two extraordinary individuals like Edison and Disney recognized the value of creativity, then certainly we need to become more creative. There is no bypassing creativity as a salesperson. It is an essential requirement now and in the years ahead.

The final component of PACT is *Trust*. Even if a person is creative, passionate, and authentic, I would never buy from him or her unless there was trust. Why do you refer a friend to your dentist or a family member to your insurance agent? You trust them. It is as simple as that.

Would you ever make a recommendation of someone you did not trust to your family or friends? I would never do this, and I am sure you feel the same way. We buy from people

> *Trust is the fundamental building block on which all human relationships are built.*

we trust. Stephen Covey said, "Trust is the glue of life. It's the most essential ingredient in effective communication. It's the foundational principle that holds all relationships." Trust is the fundamental building block on which all human relationships are built. The answer to *Would You Buy from You?* is simple when you think about it. I will gladly buy from someone I trust, and I would purchase from someone who inspires me with tremendous passion—meaning they have energy, dedication, and enthusiasm in all that they do. I am even more inclined to say *yes* when I know a person is authentic. This means they are consistent in behavior no matter the circumstances. They are real, and they focus on ethics and integrity. If a person does all of this with a creative approach, I am likely never to leave. When a PACT sales approach is in place, price is not much of a factor. When people are creative, and approach life in a unique manner, they operate with an "as if" mindset. This means they see things "as if" they can be done and are not afraid to challenge why something can't be done. When you have a PACT philosophy in sales, it is hard for a buyer to say no. They, too, are lured in by the amazing mix of energy, honesty, and uniqueness that is *all* built upon trust.

So, we have come full circle. And the question of this book must be reframed. If we follow the advice we've read about, then *Would You Buy from You?* becomes *How could you not buy from you?* And, friends, as I tell my university students, until next time... Keep Pushing Forward.

CONCLUSION:

Would You Buy from You?

Well friends, we are nearing the end of this book. So why include a conclusion? Well, I love seeing the encore performance at the end of a concert, so since I have felt you were cheering for me to come back with a few more pages, I am going to do just that. I want to review some of the things we have covered in this book and add a few more closing thoughts. As you may recall, I gave you the word *CUB* as a way to remember the main sections of this book. C = Constantly Connected, U = Under the Iceberg Mindset, and B = Brand.

The title of the book both asked us a question, *Would You Buy from You?* and also provided an answer, *Your Brand Makes the Difference.* Let's focus on the question first. We learned that to effectively sell, market, or communicate anything in today's world, we must understand

127

it and not be afraid of it. We must be open-minded to learning new things and doing things in different ways. As I said before, you are either moving forward or going backward in life. There is no such thing as staying the same. The world we live in is

> *We must be open-minded to learning new things and doing things in different ways.*

"constantly connected," and we are now more cognizant of this fact when we hear people say things like they are drowning, slammed, buried, snowed under, in the weeds, swamped, and more. It is likely you have said this in recent weeks, and I know as hard as I try not to, that I have done so as well.

The key to understanding our constantly connected world is to embrace it. Yes, that is right. You must jump right in and understand it. You must become an expert in making your messages get through the noise. And you must help those clients—who feel "slammed" to the point that they do not even know where to begin—feel comfortable taking the first steps. It is our job to be a breath of fresh air and make another person's life easier. This is what they want and need, whether they verbally say so, or not. I don't know about you, but this is the type of person I want to buy from. Note: it is a lot easier to "let a salesperson down" by telling them their price is too high. After all, why would a buyer really want to open up about the stress they feel unless they completely trust you? And you are correct and now know that it is hard to get them to be transparent and tell us what is truly going on (see Section 2). Thus, you will hear objections like *your price is too high*. It is a simple way to make you "go away" or leave them alone. And unfortunately when this occurs, we have been unsuccessful in conveying true value, so they are not going to invest any more time with us.

Once we realize the difficulty of "disconnecting," we must be proactive in how we deal with this loud and rapidly changing world. Our messages should be clear, concise, and consistent. We know the answer to the book is our "brand makes the difference." So we must think of our brand in a deliberate manner in everything we do, say, and write (online and offline) each and every day. And this is hard

> *To have the best success of getting your message through, be sure it is conveyed in a clear manner so that it's easy to understand.*

to do. To have the best success of getting your message through, be sure it is conveyed in a clear manner so that it's easy to understand. Also, keep your message concise (we live in a 140 character tweet/sound bite world). If you write long emails and letters, stop. Nobody will read them. If you leave long voicemails, become more concise. Make them more succinct and to the point. If you cannot tell someone why you do what you do in 12-17 seconds, you need to learn how, or you will lose your audience. If you are not consistent in building your brand, then you need to become consistent. If you pledge to be on certain social media channels each week, then you need to be there. If you commit to prospecting or going to a networking event on a regular basis, then make it happen. No excuses. And remember, whatever you say (in an email, in person, on the phone, via text, or through social media) should align so that your brand is consistent.

We are now aware that in 2015 and beyond it is not just a good idea to think at a deeper level; it is an absolute requirement to achieve success. We discussed that most people focus on the above-the-surface visible part of an iceberg that makes up only 10 percent of the whole, whereas 90 percent (approximately) of the iceberg is under the surface where we cannot see it and thus do not think about it. The challenge to us as salespersons and marketers is, do we really know "why" we do what we do, and why another person does what he or she does? Do we understand that this constantly connected world has caused many of us have an even shorter attention span? This means it is more likely that we will not make time to get to another's "why" or worldview. If we do not know why some feel what they feel or act as they do, how can we possibly expect to sell or market to them in an effective manner? We cannot.

Nobody on this planet has any more or any less time than another. We all have (24/7) 168 hours in a week; no more and no less. Be sure you do not let yourself or another settle for saying, "There was not enough time to get it done." Baloney. Your reply to yourself or another must be, "Yes, there was time." You just did not make time to

Time can be your greatest asset or enemy, depending on how you use it.

get something done and instead chose (yes, your choice) to do something else. So whether you are a millionaire who owns five companies, or an hourly worker at a retail store, guess what? You both have the same amount of time each day, week, and year. Thus the choice becomes what you do with your time. Time can be your greatest asset or enemy, depending on how you use it.

We discussed what a brand *is* and *is not*, and why it makes all the difference to your sales success. Your brand, if deeply valued, readily answers the questions of "So what? Why you? Who cares?" And your brand is all about value. A price is just that; a number. However, value is the sum of your price, plus your services/offerings, plus YOU. Yes, people ultimately buy something when they can see a true *value* in it. If there is no distinct difference in what you or your company offers, then a buyer's decision will likely be based on price. After all, this is only fair if we give them no other criteria to consider. Another person's perception of our brand is their reality. And our brand is not defined by what we say it is, but what *others* say it is. Our brand is the reputation and attributes that we come to be known for over many years. It is vital in a world with as many different ways to communicate as we have, with as many video phones filming what we do and people recording what we say, to be as genuine as possible. There is almost no way to avoid messing up. Trust me. However, this is part of our brand—the human

> *Value is the sum of your price, plus your services/offerings, plus YOU.*

part. Nobody wants to buy from or hear some perfectly scripted "PR" spiel. However, we do want to know the truth. America is very forgiving when we own up to the mistakes we make (and do so in a timely manner). Having a strong brand is not about *trying to be perfect*. It is not about being *almost perfect*. It is about being real; being genuine, being transparent, being honest, and being *human*.

So, be dedicated to what we defined in the book: to being "growth oriented" and thus a committed and continual learner. None of us will ever "fully arrive" on this earth as this is not our final destination. However, we must keep growing, learning, and seeking to improve while we are here. As we grow our brand, we will oftentimes mess up along the way. I certainly do and have, but I do my level best to learn from missteps, own up to them, reflect on them, and see how I can avoid them in the future. Do you?

I can remember my late grandmother telling me— when she was very sick and near the end of her life— that she wished she could go back in time and use the knowledge she had accumulated as she got older. She told me, "Ryan, it is almost a shame that by the time you have seen enough of life to have true wisdom, you are at an age where you cannot do a lot with it except impart it to others." I spent a lot of time listening to what she told me and took it to heart. And that was nearly 25 years ago, but it still rings clear in my head today. Little did she know the wisdom she was imparting to me would be part of a book that would be read all over the world.

This book's title developed over time. It came from my asking a number of groups I have spoken to "*Would You Buy from You?*" And the answer kept coming back as "Umm...Well...I think so... What do you mean?" You get the idea. Again, if you would

> *If you would not buy from you, then why in the world would anyone else buy from you? The answer is quite simple. They won't.*

not buy from you, then why in the world would anyone else buy from you? The answer is quite simple. They won't. It all became very clear for me while working on this book. Over time, some of the concepts came to life while I was in different parts of the country. One time it may have been while I was speaking and someone asked a question. Another time it may have been during an in-the-field sales call with one of my clients. Or it may have been a question that came up while I was teaching a class. Most recently, my 12-year-old (middle daughter), who is a gifted communicator, explained her reasoning to me regarding how she used her Instagram (photo social media account). She, like her sisters, has her name reserved on her social media accounts (they have a good branding advisor). Her Instagram name is her full name (left out for privacy), and she has a lot of followers for a 12-year-old. She, however, also has another account that is her name, but with an underscore added between her first and last name. She told me she had reserved this early on so another person would not take it, and she calls this her *backup* account. I asked her *why* she did this, and she told me that her main account is followed a lot more overall by kids of different ages. So, when she wants to post a big event/story, she will post it to her main account. However, her backup account has a good but much smaller following. So she uses that medium to get out pictures and info to subgroups, but it does not go to all. She also told me she felt the need to protect her *name,* or in my words, *brand,* so she got the one with the underscore to control both before someone else did. I will leave it at that, but I was amazed at her deep "why" level thought process of what she was doing and why she was doing it. And she did this all on her own. My daughter knows at a young age how her brand makes the difference.

> *A brand can be defined as a PACT, which answers the question of this book. P is for* Passion. *A is for* Authenticity. *C is for* Creativity, *and T is for* Trust.

A brand can be defined as a PACT, which answers the question of this book. P is for *Passion.* A is for *Authenticity.* C is for *Creativity,* and T is for *Trust.* Let's start at the end. You would never, nor would I, buy from someone you did not trust. Trust is the cornerstone of all strong human relationships. Once trust is established, we must be creative in how we approach sales situations. We talked about taking the road less traveled (a *zig-zag* sales mindset) and engaging in "as if" thinking. Don't be afraid to try something that has never been done before. Courage in creativity is when something special happens. And we must be authentic in our sales efforts. This means being true to ourselves no matter who is watching, and when nobody is watching. Such a genuine approach is what people desire when purchasing something. We must also exhibit a tremendous amount of passion. Our energy, dedication, drive, excitement, and enthusiasm make people want to be around us. It makes them want to sign on the dotted line. It makes them want to jump onboard and buy in. Passion is fun and exhilarating, and when mixed with the other three ingredients, you have the perfect PACT.

So, we started off on a journey to answer the question, "*Would You Buy from You.*" We have looked at a number of different concepts and ideas. At the end of the day, you have one advantage that nobody else on this planet has. Only

> *Our energy, dedication, drive, excitement, and enthusiasm make people want to be around us.*

you are *you.* Nobody else, no matter how hard they try, can be you. God has made you in His image and as a special creation. I challenge you to seize hold of this gift, and intentionally work on growing your brand each day so it will move in the direction you desire. Remember, as human beings we are a work in progress. It is the same with our brands. No matter where you are today, it is time to get started. Time (your 168 hours a week) is ticking away. I challenge you to *find a way* in all that you come across in life, and *make things happen.* Be a part of the solution, not part of the problem. We are at the end of the encore (lighters down please), and the question has flipped on its head from "*Would You Buy from You*" to "*How Could You Not Buy from You*? Your Brand (indeed) Makes the Difference.

About the Author

Ryan T. Sauers is President/Owner of Sauers Consulting Strategies. The firm consults with privately held organizations across North America. The areas of focus are: sales growth, brand positioning, organizational strategy, and integrated marketing (including an emphasis on social media). Ryan speaks at events across the country and writes a number of feature articles in national publications and blogs. He is an adjunct university professor teaching leadership, communication, marketing, and entrepreneurship. Ryan is a Certified Myers Briggs (MBTI), Certified Marketing Executive (SMEI) and DiSC human behavior specialist. Sauers has a Master's degree on Organizational Leadership and is working on his Doctoral degree in Organizational Leadership. Ryan is author of the best-selling book *Everyone is in Sales*. Sauers also owns two large magazines in the metro Atlanta (GA) area where he is Publisher/Owner. More info online at: RyanSauers.com, @RyanSauers, Linkedin.Com/in/RyanSauers, YouTube.com/RyanTSauers, Facebook.com/SauersConsulting, OurTownGwinnett.com

Made in the USA
Middletown, DE
27 September 2015